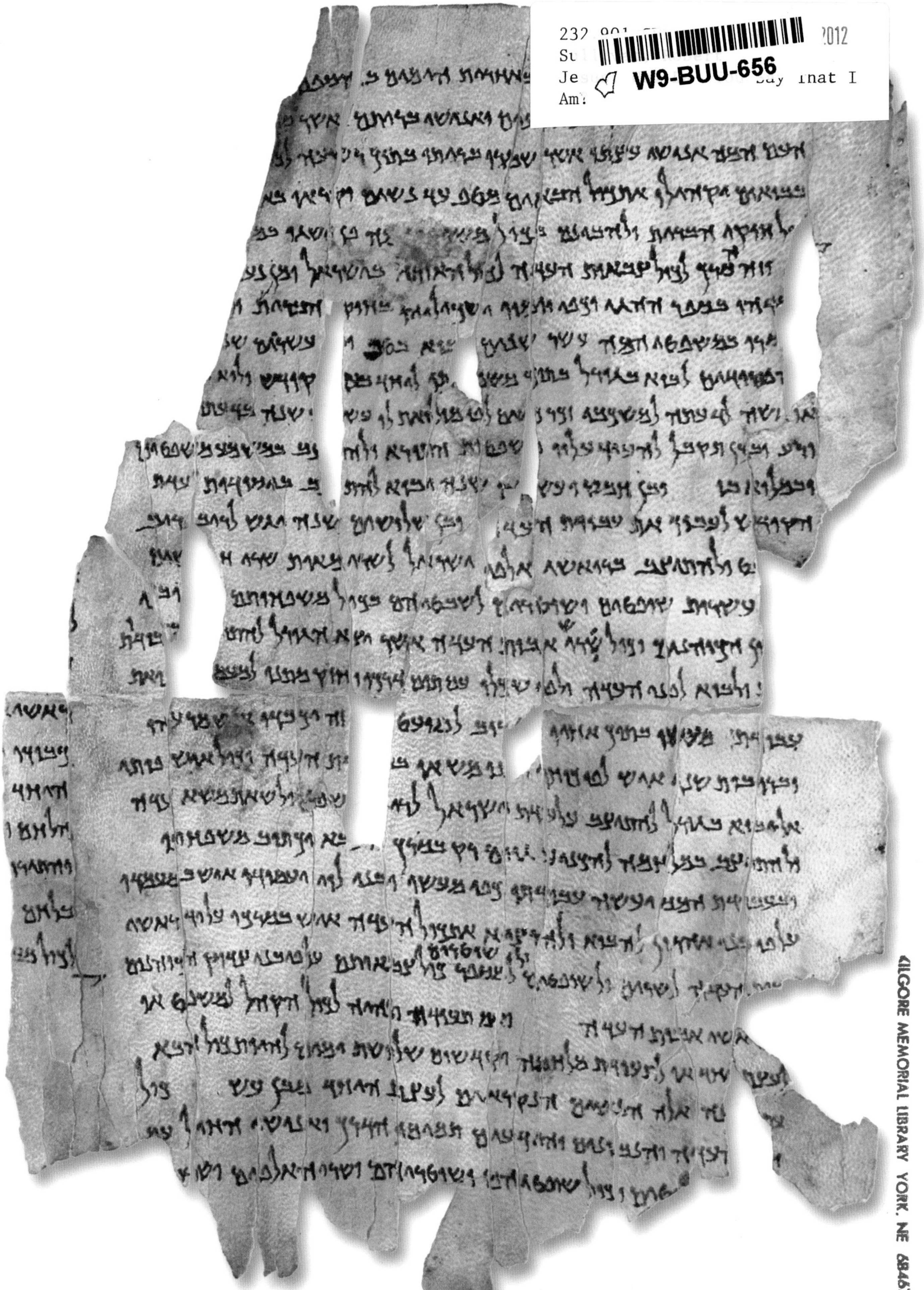

JESUS

Who Do You Say That I Am?

TABLE OF CONTENTS

LIFE BOOKS

Managing Editor Robert Sullivan
Director of Photography Barbara Baker Burrows
Creative Director Mimi Park
Deputy Picture Editor Christina Lieberman
Copy Chief Barbara Gogan
Copy Editors Don Armstrong, Parlan McGaw
Writer-Reporters Marilyn Fu, Amy Lennard Goehner
Photo Associate Sarah Cates
Consulting Picture Editors
Mimi Murphy (Rome), Tala Skari (Paris)

Editorial Director Stephen Koepp
Editorial Operations Director Michael Q. Bullerdick

EDITORIAL OPERATIONS

Richard K. Prue (Director), Brian Fellows (Manager),
Richard Shaffer (Production), Keith Aurelio,
Charlotte Coco, Kevin Hart, Mert Kerimoglu,
Rosalie Khan, Patricia Koh, Marco Lau, Brian Mai,
Po Fung Ng, Rudi Papiri, Robert Pizaro, Barry Pribula,
Clara Renauro, Katy Saunders, Hia Tan, Vaune Trachtman

TIME HOME ENTERTAINMENT

Publisher Jim Childs
Vice President, Business Development & Strategy
Steven Sandonato
Executive Director, Marketing Services Carol Pittard
Executive Director, Retail & Special Sales Tom Mifsud
Executive Publishing Director Joy Butts
Director, Bookazine Development & Marketing
Laura Adam
Finance Director Glenn Buonocore
Associate Publishing Director Megan Pearlman
Assistant General Counsel Helen Wan
Assistant Director, Special Sales Ilene Schreider
Book Production Manager Suzanne Janso
Design & Prepress Manager Anne-Michelle Gallero
Brand Manager Roshni Patel
Associate Prepress Manager Alex Voznesenskiy
Assistant Brand Manager Stephanie Braga

Special thanks: Christine Austin, Katherine Barnet,
Jeremy Biloon, Susan Chodakiewicz, Rose Cirrincione,
Lauren Hall Clark, Jacqueline Fitzgerald, Christine Font,
Jenna Goldberg, Hillary Hirsch, David Kahn,
Amy Mangus, Robert Marasco, Kimberly Marshall,
Amy Migliaccio, Nina Mistry, Dave Rozzelle,
Adriana Tierno, Vanessa Wu

ISBN 10: 1-60320-174-2
ISBN 13: 978-1-60320-174-2
Library of Congress Control Number: 2010941156

"LIFE" is a registered trademark of Time Inc.

We welcome your comments and suggestions about
LIFE Books. Please write to us at: LIFE Books,
Attention: Book Editors, PO Box 11016,
Des Moines, IA 50336-1016

If you would like to order any of our hardcover Collector's
Edition books, please call us at 1-800-327-6388
(Monday through Friday, 7:00 a.m.–8:00 p.m.
or Saturday, 7:00 a.m.–6:00 p.m. Central Time).

ENDPAPERS: THE SCROLL OF THE RULE, PHOTOGRAPH BY WEST SEMITIC
RESEARCH/DEAD SEA SCROLLS FOUNDATION/CORBIS
PAGE 1: MOUNT SINAI, PHOTOGRAPH BY PETER WILSON/AXIOM/AURORA
PAGES 2–3: MICHELANGELO'S "PIETÀ," PHOTOGRAPH BY ARNOLD NEWMAN
THESE PAGES: THE SEA OF GALILEE, PHOTOGRAPH BY DENIS WAUGH

THE CARPENTER'S SON WHO CHANGED EVERYTHING

The great artist and scientist Leonardo da Vinci imagined Jesus in his painting "Head of Christ," made near the end of the 15th century (left). Many thousands of others have imagined Him—or thought they were actually seeing Him—when gazing upon the Shroud of Turin (right), which they believe to be the burial shroud of Jesus with His bloodstained image imprinted upon it. Was this Him? Does it matter? Is it enough to see Jesus, however He appears to us, in prayer, or in dreams? Do we need to see Him to follow Him?

ROM THE MOST MODEST OF means in a volatile part of the world that people of varying faiths (including the three great monotheisms—Judaism, Christianity and Islam) would come to call the Holy Land, a young man emerged whose radical, inspiring philosophy seemed not only a challenge to religious orthodoxy and political authority, but perhaps a course forward through life, which was so often a vale of tears. He developed a following, and after His martyrdom, when He was barely 30 years of age, a cult. What would become the world's largest religion grew in the shadows and clandestine "churches" of the pagan Roman Empire, until finally the empire, *not* the dissidents who regularly sacrificed life and liberty for their beliefs, yielded.

Who was this man?

For many, He was an answer to what had been prophesied by the sages—the fulfillment of a promise made. He was, for others, a different kind of answer—the alternative was despair. For still others, His words seemed to present the answers to life's very biggest questions. He seemed, to them, "the way."

In this LIFE book, in words and pictures, is the story of Jesus of Nazareth, presented with historical context: what came before, what Jesus meant in His time, what He means in ours today. It's a story that has been related a million times and many more than that, sometimes with bias. (The Gospel writers, certainly, had a bias: a reason for writing as persuasively as they did.) It has been called, famously, the greatest story ever told.

The story is a response to a challenge posed by Jesus Himself: "But who do you say that I am?" Later, speaking of his own mission but clearly of divinity as well, Paul attempted an answer: "All things to all men."

He was right at the time. He is right today.

To some, Jesus is the Son of God, the anointed,

the Christ—born to a virgin just more than 2,000 years ago (perhaps, say a consensus of historians, around 4 B.C.). To others Jesus is just a man, albeit a man who spurred, through His teachings and exemplary life, several faiths now incorporated into Christianity. And to still others He is little more than a myth. Maybe He lived, they say, but His stature as a great and transcendent human being is a novelistic invention of Paul and, then, the Gospel writers, who required a charismatic anchor for their nascent churches. He is, say these naysayers, an idea.

But . . .

Whether idea or man, Jesus—in whose name, surely, wars have been fought, and awful deeds done—is a model that, day to day, encourages

The hands of an Orthodox Christian priest are covered with mud after being dipped in the Jordan River before the annual ritual blessing of the waters at the baptismal site of Qasr al-Yahud near the West Bank city of Jericho. John the Baptist anointed Jesus in the Jordan, and many pilgrims venture there today to know Him better.

much good, a mirror that reflects, for many of us, our hopes. We see Jesus as many different people—dutiful son, ascetic, revolutionary, sage, martyr—depending on our personal beliefs and, indeed, our personal needs. A great many of us, Christians and not, want Jesus on our team. We want to be His teammate. We want to be like Him. We want Him to be like us.

Consider, however: If Jesus existed—and although some see Him principally as a Pauline invention, Jesus all but certainly *did* exist—then He must have looked Semitic. But the masterpieces of European religious art did not portray Him that way, as you already know and will note again when looking at these pages. The Africans know a dark-skinned Jesus, the Swedes a blond one, the Chinese an Asiatic Jesus; Americans picture the bearded Jesus of a billion prayer-book covers. We see Jesus in our own image. It helps us to know Him better. To understand Him. It helps us to hear Him speak, when we read His sayings rendered in the poetic, if archaic, words of the King James version of the Bible—poetic words that hum familiarly from childhood, but that have mature, profound, undeniable power.

Contemplating all this—our Jesus among many Jesuses—may help us come to understand Him better.

It may help us, too, to know what others think of Him: not only historical figures of certain importance—famous philosophers, the Gospel scribes, long-gone poets and balladeers, our country's founding fathers—but also contemporary figures of scholarship or renown. LIFE's editors have interviewed, over the course of the past several years, eminent thinkers, including historians, theologians and clergy. We have talked, as well, to prominent public personalities who have had some good cause to contemplate Jesus—His life, His deeds, what He stands for, what He means to them and what He means, perhaps, to us all. Various insights and impressions are reflected in these pages.

The testimony of these diverse witnesses makes one point clear: Whether Jesus was sent from Heaven or not, whether He died on the cross or not, and ascended or did not—Jesus is alive in our time. To believers and nonbelievers alike, Jesus matters. Still matters. He long has. He always will.

TURKEY

Ephesus

Athens
Corinth
Malta
Rome

Mediterranean Sea

CYPRUS

LEBANON

SYRIA

ISRAEL

Jerusalem

GOSHEN

EGYPT
(SINAI)

JORDAN

Cairo

Petra

EGYPT

Nile River

Mount
Sinai

SAUDI
ARABIA

Red Sea

THE WORLD OF JESUS

This part of the Middle East, Europe and Asia has been drawn and redrawn since biblical times: The Mesopotamians and Goshens and Canaans no longer exist, but new nations have arisen to take their place. What you need to know as you approach Jesus: The land that both Muslims and Jews see as "promised," and that Christians and all people believe nurtured not only Jesus of Nazareth but, subsequently, the seeds of Christianity, was largely in Canaan,

today's Lebanon, Jordan, Israel and the West Bank). When the Twelve Tribes of Israel split, according to Judaism's Torah (which underlies the Christian Old Testament), Solomon's kingdom was divided. Israel to the north became independent of Judah to the south. As regards the New Testament: Nazareth and the Galilean territory where Jesus's mission got started is to the north in the smaller map; Judaea and its capital, Jerusalem, is to the south; and the Judaean wilder-

PROPHETS

In the Aramaic language there is a root word meaning "fruitful, well watered" that is often associated with the name of Eden. It has been used as one of several clues by those who would place Eden in the land of the Tigris (opposite) and Euphrates rivers. There is, however, no archaeological evidence; and where one places Eden and what one makes of what transpired there, is, like so much in the Bible, dependent upon interpretation and, more important still, faith.

OW TO START? THE BOOK OF Genesis would seem an easy place and would provide the perfect quoted passage: "In the beginning . . ." And, in fact, that is the way to start: with the story of what occurred before the boy was born to the carpenter Joseph and his wife, Mary. That history was written by divinely inspired authors between two and three millennia ago, and represents the holy scripture of Judaism; it is included in a sacred volume, the Tanakh, which is an acronym of its triadic parts—the Torah (or "Law," or "Pentateuch"); Nevi'im ("Prophets"); and Ketuvim ("writings"). Others (among them biblical scholars) call the Tanakh "the Hebrew Bible," considering this a neutral term for portions of the Jewish and Christian canons that are held in common. (The largest part of the Christian Old Testament is drawn from the Tanakh.)

Any designation besides Tanakh would displease many Jews; the word "bible," which is derived from the Greek biblia ("the books"), doesn't even have a precise translation in Hebrew. Still, "the Hebrew Bible" or "the Hebrew Scriptures" would be more acceptable than "the Old Testament," which wouldn't even exist as a term except in the context of a New Testament. This second testament concerns itself, of course, with the life and

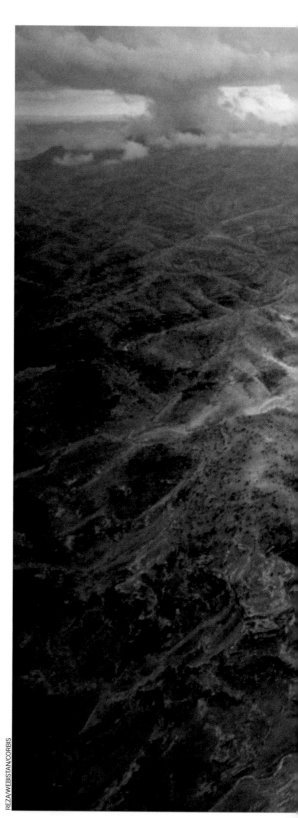

teachings of Jesus, who is claimed in the Gospels of the New Testament to be the Son of God. The New Testament's argument is contrary to Jewish thought, which maintains that the Savior is yet to come.

But the fact remains that the narratives and teachings of the Tanakh correspond closely with those of the Old Testament. (At least, with the Protestant Christian version. The Old Testaments in Roman Catholic and Orthodox Bibles have material found nowhere in the Tanakh.) We say "correspond closely," and that's careful wording. When the early Christians were assembling their book in the century after Christ's crucifixion, they accepted the Jewish view of history as truth—with reservations. Working from a Greek translation of the Tanakh rather than from the Hebrew text, they incorporated nuanced changes that would prove crucial (for instance, the mother of the Messiah would be "a young woman," says the Hebrew word *almah*, but the Greek *parthenos* stipulates "a virgin"). Some chapters were reordered or ignored; some episodes sacred to Jews diminished.

The first sections of both the Tanakh and the Old Testament set forth religious and social rules. They tell the story of the creation and describe the Lord's covenant with Israel, the Exodus from Egypt and the Hebrew people's arrival in the Promised Land. The dominant personalities in these early chapters include Abraham, the great shared patriarch of the three monotheistic religions (again: Judaism,

Noah, seen below in a 13th-century illustration made by an anonymous monk in Akko, Kingdom of Jerusalem, existed so long ago that his narrative—however much of it actually occurred—predates even the timeline on the bottom of these pages. This makes sense, of course, because the inundation of the Holy Land would have had to occur well before the Hebrew migration from Mesopotamia to Canaan. If indeed Noah's ark settled "upon the mountains of Ararat," as scripture has it, did this indicate Mount Ararat in Turkey (opposite)? That it might have, has been the rationale (or hope) behind hundreds of searches throughout the centuries. Again, acceptance of the flood tradition, as with Adam and Eve in Paradise, must be based on a belief system. And that is fine, because even believers are quick to accept that physical proof may be eternally unavailable.

Before Christ

2000 B.C.	1900	1800	1700	1600	1500	1400	1300	1200	1100	1000

THE HEBREWS

Philistines invade

Migration from Mesopotamia to Canaan — *In Egypt* — *To Canaan* — *Tribes federate* — *Kingdom formed*

PATRIARCHS — EXODUS — JUDGES

ABRAHAM — MOSES JOSHUA — SAMSON SAUL DAVID / SAMUEL / SOLOMON

THEIR RULERS AND ADVERSARIES

MESOPOTAMIA	EGYPT	CANAAN-AMMON-MOAB-PHILISTIA

III DYNASTY OF UR — OLD BABYLONIAN KINGDOM — HAMMURABI — HYKSOS DYNASTY — THUTMOSE III — SETI I — RAMSES II / MERNEPTAH

We have traveled two millennia since the time of Christ. Two millennia and more of biblical—religious—history came before His Advent. Here is a graphic look at several of the many important historical figures, episodes and movements that roiled the Holy Land for century upon century, building the story that would, eventually, include Jesus of Nazareth. Much of this is detailed or commented upon in the Torah; the pre-Jesus narrative has been filled out, subsequently, by historians and archaeologists. This timeline is perhaps useful as we ponder the questions: What led to Jesus? What role did He fill?

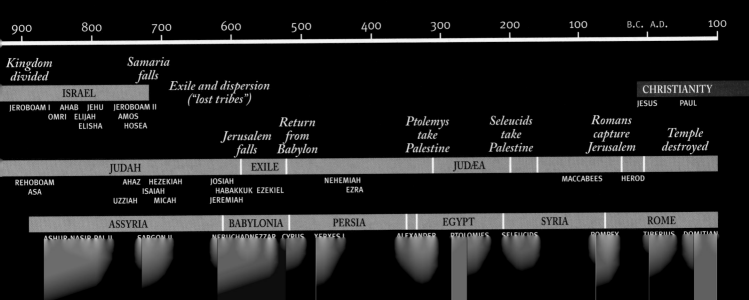

900	800	700	600	500	400	300	200	100	B.C. A.D.	100

Kingdom divided

Samaria falls

Exile and dispersion ("lost tribes")

ISRAEL

CHRISTIANITY

JEROBOAM I   AHAB   JEHU   JEROBOAM II
OMRI   ELIJAH   AMOS
ELISHA   HOSEA

JESUS   PAUL

Return from Babylon

Jerusalem falls

Ptolemys take Palestine

Seleucids take Palestine

Romans capture Jerusalem

Temple destroyed

JUDAH   **EXILE**   **JUDÆA**

REHOBOAM   AHAZ   HEZEKIAH   JOSIAH   NEHEMIAH
ASA   ISAIAH   HABAKKUK EZEKIEL   EZRA
UZZIAH   MICAH   JEREMIAH

MACCABEES   HEROD

ASSYRIA   **BABYLONIA**   **PERSIA**   **EGYPT**   **SYRIA**   **ROME**

ASHUR-NASIR-PAL II   SARGON II   NEBUCHADNEZZAR CYRUS   XERXES I   ALEXANDER   PTOLOMIES   SELEUCIDS   POMPEY   TIBERIUS   DOMITIAN

Christianity and Islam), and then, of course, Moses. The second section, "Prophets," recounts the Israeli history in Palestine, and is filled not only with prophecies but with wars and heroes—principal among the latter, David. "Writings" includes meditations on evil and death, as well as psalms and praises of Israel's covenant with God.

And so, in the beginning, the world was created, and on the seventh day God rested. Eden was home to Adam and Eve, God's perfect man and woman, who, tempted by the serpent, ate of the forbidden fruit and thus fell from grace with God. Through their disobedience, Adam and Eve introduced sin to the world; in essence, they shattered Paradise. Conflict—bloody conflict—arrived with humankind's very next generation, when Adam and Eve's son Cain slew his brother Abel, then lied to God about the act ("Am I my brother's keeper?"). Violence, of course, permeates the world still. It is an obvious and harsh irony that in a land once Edenic (various geographical markers in Genesis place Eden in the Holy Land for most interpreters) war rages today—and has raged, off and on, for much of history.

Opposite: In a 15th-century depiction by the Italian Bonifacio Bembo, Abraham's hand is stayed by an angel of the Lord before he can slay his son Isaac. Below, in the Dome of the Rock shrine in Jerusalem, is the area of stone believed to have been used by Abraham as he prepared his sacrifice. Bembo's painting was meant to edify Christians and the shrine is, of course, holy to Muslims, too, and indicates Abraham's important place in both religions (though, as will be elucidated, they differ on details of what actually happened to which son way back when). The third great monotheistic faith, Judaism, also regards Abraham as a patriarch; he is the meeting point for religions that all too often refuse to meet.

GARY BRAASCH/CORBIS

RICHARD T. NOWITZ

The son of Lamech was named Noah, whom God looked upon as "a just man," and entrusted with nothing less than the salvation of his race, once the Lord, seeing a planet "filled with violence," had decided: "I will destroy man whom I have created from the face of the earth, both man and beast . . . for it repenteth me that I have made them." God said to Noah, "Make thee an ark of gopher wood . . . I, even I, do bring a flood of waters upon the earth, to destroy all flesh, wherein is the breath of life, from under heaven; and every thing that is in the earth shall die. But with thee will I establish my covenant; and thou shalt come into the ark, thou, and thy sons, and thy wife, and thy sons' wives with thee. And of every living thing of all flesh, two of every sort shalt thou bring into the ark, to keep them alive with thee; they shall be male and female."

Noah did as instructed, and he, his family and their large menagerie "went in two and two"—then saw the rains come. "And the rain was upon the earth forty days and forty nights." The flooding

We have emphasized, as we looked at earlier pictures of the Tigris River and Mount Ararat, that physical evidence of biblical stories is often speculative. However, throughout the Holy Land there are many, many man-made tributes to the power, influence and glory—the reality, then and now—of the prophets: tributes to Abraham, to Moses (as we will soon see) and, on these pages, to Jesus, who was indeed considered a great prophet even by those who did not think Him to be the Son of God. The men who built the 5th-century Great Laura of Mar Saba monastery in the Judaean Desert, in what is now the Israeli

occupied West Bank, certainly did believe in Jesus's divinity. Founded by Saint Sabas, it is today the oldest monastery of the Greek Orthodox faith, and within its walls were developed many of the religious customs of the Christian Orthodoxies. The monastery remains a living, breathing organism—no relic— with some 20 monks in residence. While arguments between Muslims and Jews in the Holy Land make the nightly news, and Christian influence in the region has dwindled to insignificance, the religious work of each faith, based upon the words and deeds of the prophets, goes on.

lasted even longer, and Noah's ark was borne upon the waves. Finally, "God made a wind to pass over the earth, and the waters asswaged"—causing the ark to settle "upon the mountains of Ararat." Eventually the flood subsided, and Noah and his kin and their many animals exited the ark. The story of mankind would be allowed to progress.

A 10th-generation descendant of Noah was born, sometime between 2100 and 1500 B.C. in the Mesopotamian city of Ur of the Chaldees. He was given a name, Abram, meaning "father love," or an exaltation of the father.

Ur in the time of Abram's upbringing would hardly have been a godless place—it would have been a many-godded place, a polytheistic city. Most of Ur looked up to a moon god named Sin, but other deities abounded. How Abram's thinking evolved

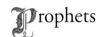

SCALA/ART RESOURCE, NY

For Jews, Moses remains the titanic prophet, and his life certainly was filled with titanic episodes. At left, in a painting by the 15th-century artist Cosimo Rosselli that is today in the Vatican's Sistine Chapel, the pursuing Egyptians are engulfed by the Red Sea after Moses and his Israelites have crossed over during the Exodus. Opposite, below: The sun appears on the rocky horizon at Mount Sinai in Egypt, believed by many to be the peak where Moses received the Ten Commandments from Jehovah. Below, left: Moses brandishing the tablets in a famed 17th-century painting by Rembrandt. Below: The room in Tel Shilo, Israel, where, it is said, the Ark of the Covenant, housing the Commandments, was once kept.

RICHARD T. NOWITZ

BPK, BERLIN/STAATLICHE MUSEEN/JOERG P. ANDERS/ART RESOURCE, NY

The kings David and Solomon, seen at left in a 14th-century mosaic on the south wall of the ante-baptistry in Venice's Saint Mark's Basilica, personified courage, might and wisdom as they forwarded the Hebrew story—and pointed directly to Jesus in the Christian telling. As with the life of Mary's divine son, the narrative was progressing from Bethlehem through the Judaean wilderness to, fatefully, Jerusalem. Below is the western

wall of the temple built by Solomon, destroyed by the Babylonians in 586 B.C. and restored circa 515 B.C. It was rebuilt by Herod the Great, in the employ of the Roman Empire, in the 1st century B.C., and the doorways here, which opened onto shops in the temple wall, would have been seen by Mary and Joseph when they visited the city with their child. Right: Jerusalem, dominated by Solomon's Temple, in a map imagined much later, in 1846.

ERICH LESSING/ART RESOURCE, NY

BUYENLARGE/GETTY

to monotheism—and thereby put him in a position to become the first patriarch of both the people of Israel and the Arabs—is speculative. What is known is that the Hebrew Tanakh, the Christian Bible and Islam's Koran all agree: Abram was a believer in one god, *the* God, and was given by God an assignment to travel far and wide, eventually to a land where a great nation would be founded. In return for going, said God, "I will bless thee, and make thy name great; and thou shalt be a blessing: And I will bless them that bless thee, and curse him that curseth thee: and in thee shall all families of the earth be blessed." When God made Abram's name great, He changed it to Abraham—father of nations.

To greatly simplify the latter chapters of Abraham's story, and to explain, in brief, the split between Judaism and Islam: In Genesis, God tested Abraham's faith by asking him to sacrifice his son Isaac. Abraham was on the verge of doing so atop Mount Moriah when God stayed his hand. "Saith the Lord, for because thou hast done this thing, and hast not withheld thy son, thine only son: That in blessing I will bless thee," an angel

told Abraham. "[A]nd in multiplying I will multiply thy seed as the stars of the heaven, and as the sand which is upon the sea shore; and thy seed shall possess the gate of his enemies; And in thy seed shall all the nations of the earth be blessed; because thou hast obeyed my voice." This prophecy will lead quickly to Isaac's son Jacob—and thus to Israel. And in the Christian version, to Jesus.

This is the earliest example of God selecting Jerusalem as the setting in which a crucial drama would unfold; it is to be His city of special purpose. After the angel proclaimed, it provided a ram as a substitute sacrifice. Isaac was allowed to grow, prosper and, through his own son Jacob (who would be called Israel), to found the Jewish nation in Palestine. But according to Islam, it was Ishmael, the other Abrahamic son, who was nearly sacrificed. His many offspring settled on the site of the future Mecca, south of Abraham's land in what is now Saudi Arabia. There, they flourished, spreading across the Arab world: The Muslims, now 1.6 billion strong, today represent the largest religion save Christianity.

Abraham died, according to scripture, at age 175 and was buried beside his wife in the Cave of Machpelah, east of Mamre. (Jews honor their heritage there, in the West Bank, at Hebron's Tomb of the Patriarchs, where Abraham, Sarah, Isaac and Isaac's son Jacob are said to rest.)

Much more happened through the centuries, and many more prophets came to prominence: Jacob fled Canaan for Mesopotamia, where he was taken in by his mother's brother Laban. Then Jacob was the victim of treachery: He agreed to work seven years for Laban if his reward was the wife he desired, Rachel. At the end of the seven-year period, Laban gave him Rachel's sister Leah, instead; Jacob had to toil another seven years to gain Rachel, too. By his wives and two concubines, Jacob would father 12 sons and a daughter. The boys, as men, would become heads of the Twelve Tribes of Israel—the 11th son, his father's favorite, was Joseph, whose primacy created great unrest, which doesn't really pertain to this story.

Nor does Joseph's time in Egypt and rise to prominence in the pharaoh's kingdom—except that he had his family promise that his remains would one day be buried back in Canaan, thus reestablishing the notion of Israel's Holy Land. Joseph would die in Egypt at age 110, but his wish would be fulfilled, perhaps as many as 400 years later, when Moses made sure to bring along Joseph's bones during the Exodus.

Moshe Rabbenu (Moses Our Teacher) was, to Jews, the lawgiver, hero above all heroes; to Christians, Moses, a model of faith; to Muslims, Musa, the first prophet to herald the coming of Muhammad. He is said to have lived some 3,200 years ago in the time of Egyptian pharaoh Ramses II. Proving his existence has, as with Abraham and the other patriarchs, been impossible. Some scholars have pointed out that several chapters in the Moses saga, beginning with the story of a baby in an ark woven of reeds, are similar to older Mesopotamian and Egyptian legends. So what? Even if Moses or aspects of him were borrowed, there are in his story entirely original philosophies, and these endure (indeed, sometimes endure through Jesus or Muhammad, who would deliver modifications of Moses's teachings).

Moses, crucially (and as a model for Jesus), seems real, and the detail and complexity of his depiction—right down to a speech impediment—may be the

strongest argument that such a man did exist. Moses is exceedingly human: weak and strong, brave yet tormented by doubt, a rebel but a faithful follower. "The most solitary and most powerful hero in biblical history," Elie Wiesel called Moses. "After him, nothing else was the same again."

That is certainly true. Among his life's many titanic episodes, Moses would be the receptor of God's commandments—seemingly almost cowritten by the two of them—and the thinking inherent in these laws would be echoed in the mind-set of the world's subsequent religious philosophers, from Jesus to Muhammad to Buddha to Gandhi and even great figures in our own country, such as Rev. Martin Luther King Jr. We should not kill? That's a commandment? We should love ourselves no more than we love our neighbor? Really?

Really. This kind of thinking entered the world when God spoke to Moses.

Later came another great prophet, Joshua, who began his career as an aide to Moses . . . and then came Saul . . . and then David—and all of these monumental figures were doing what would eventually be said, by Christians, of John the Baptist: preparing the way for the Lord. David entered Saul's service first as a lyre player retained to assuage the king's despondency, then as a warrior—a role in which he succeeded splendidly. David's dramatic life story would have its climactic episodes in the Judaean capital of Jerusalem, but it began on the hillsides of Bethlehem, an outlying town where shepherds tended their flocks. Sound familiar? That, of course, is no accident. There are many echoes from the Old Testament in the New, and this is not only because, in Christian belief, Jesus is the answer to many prophecies. It is to tie Him to a lineage of great heroes. In this case, the tie is firm and formal: Christians feel Jesus is directly descended from David, and Jews feel the coming Messiah will be descended from him. Clearly, along with Abraham and Moses, David, second king of Israel, is to be considered one of the greatest of great figures in the Hebrew Bible. From his eventual headquarters in Jerusalem, David drove the Philistines back into Philistia, conquered several Canaanite cities and expanded Israel's reach and power. David made Israel great. Then the warrior king was succeeded by a philosopher king, Solomon—a peace lover, hoping to guide his nation with an "understanding heart." It was said

In the panoramic view of the Old City in Jerusalem below, the close proximity of the Western Wall, sacred to Jews, and the Islamic Dome of the Rock can be appreciated. The Mount of Olives and the Gethsemane garden, which would feature so strongly in the Christian story, are just as close by. The prophecies insisted: Jerusalem is the place. Other locales— Bethlehem, Nazareth, Galilee, Medina, Mecca, all of Canaan, all of Palestine—would be important. But, always, eternally: Jerusalem.

In the time before Jesus and soon after His Advent, much was written about all of the dramatic happenings in the Holy Land, then and in times of yore. Certainly with Jesus becoming news—and with Him being recognized as the embodiment of the Good News by those who would forward Christianity— the writing was feverish. Not all of it made it into the Bible, to be sure. We have always known this, but in modern times the truth has become self-evident, and has forced a more nuanced reading of the Old and New Testaments. The most famous discovery of apocryphal texts came in 1947 in the caves above the ruins of the ancient settlement at Qumran, Israel (below), where the Essenes, a sect of Jewish scribes, had stored their accounts. Jesus was present in the so-called Dead Sea Scrolls (opposite, a segment being examined) but not necessarily the precise same Jesus we knew from the biblical Gospels. The story as handed down by the prophets did not so much become confused as more complicated—more intriguing.

RICHARD T. NOWITZ

LARRY BURROWS

that he wrote 3,000 wise parables and 1,500 lovely poems; most of the book of Proverbs is attributed to him, as is the sensual Song of Songs ("thy love is better than wine . . .").

Solomonic wisdom and glory came to be reflected in the king's palace complex and in the temple. David had kept the Ark of the Covenant, which contained the Ten Commandments, in a tent; Solomon, beginning in the fourth year of his reign and not finishing until the 11th, erected for it a magnificent house of worship. This First Temple in Jerusalem was destroyed by the Babylonians in 586 B.C. A new temple would be built almost five centuries later by a king in service to the Roman Empire whose name you know: Herod.

And so God's way and an evolving moral code had been established through these many historical figures. The whole of the story awaited, now, the Messiah.

It awaited the man who, much of the world has long believed, was Jesus.

UNTO YOU IS BORN THIS DAY

OW DO WE KNOW OF JESUS? IN the past several decades, we have learned much more about Him from discoveries such as the Dead Sea Scrolls and ever-deeper scholarship into the Gnostic Gospels—early narratives concerning His life that were excluded from the Bible by the Christians who first decided what to include and what to omit.

But what most of us think we know of Him comes from the New Testament: This is the bedrock upon which the world's largest religion—there are more than 2.2 billion Christians today—is based. It is, if you will, the official biography.

At 27 books, it constitutes a far shorter narrative than does the Old Testament; it's about a quarter as long. But then, it covers only a bit more than 30 years, not 30-plus millennia. The first four books, called Gospels (from the Anglo-Saxon *god-spell*, or "good news"), sketch the life of Jesus, son of a Jewish carpenter and his wife . . . but also: Jesus, Son of God. This fact changed the entire message of the Old Testament. Christ was the Messiah. All that came before was leading to Him, not to some still-prophesied savior. He was and is the one.

Why were the Gnostic Gospels—52 texts in all, written from the 2nd through the 4th centuries—including famous narratives such as that of Thomas, excluded by the compilers of the New Testament, and why were those of Mark, Matthew, Luke and John included? Because the men behind the New Testament's disparate elements intended from the very first to build a religion, or at least a following, a fraternity of faith. They were adherents of the teachings of a recently executed prophet and healer whose altogether original philosophy—if it was Moses-based, it still went further—had already proved attractive to many, especially the poor or the otherwise marginalized. Turn the other cheek, said Jesus. And: Give the beggar your cloak. Love thy neighbor as thyself. Remarkable.

The writers behind the New Testament and the subsequent editors who decided the authorized version of the Bible were true believers in the words they were ascribing to the one they called the Christ (the Greek word *christos* equates with "oil," and so Jesus was "the anointed one"). Operating under the Roman radar lest they face imprisonment or death, they were first an outlaw cult, then something of a sect. The leaders of this slowly spreading fellowship were proselytizers and evangelists, preaching behind closed doors, writing down their historical accounts and interpretations. And trying to keep their message, in a confusing time, as clear as possible.

Principal among them was Paul, who before his conversion had been Saul, a Jew and an enthusiastic persecutor of Jesus's earliest followers. He is the second most important figure in the rise of Christianity after Jesus himself. Once Paul heard his personal call to Christ, he became zealous in bringing the message to the world—the Romans, the Corinthians, the Galatians—through sermons and epistles.

He was parsing Jesus's lessons in long, impassioned letters even before the Gospel writers were putting forth the biography. It is generally accepted, now, that Mark's Gospel was written first, and that Matthew and Luke were aware not only of the traditions upon which it was built but of the work itself. Still, there are discrepancies among the accounts: Mark doesn't report on Jesus's birth at all, for instance, while Luke and Matthew can't agree on the details—putting Mary and Joseph in different places at different times for different reasons. John's Gospel is another matter altogether, at every turn concerned with establishing Jesus's spirituality as well as His humanity.

All of this writing and much more began to take place about 25 years after Christ's death and continued for many decades—not necessarily with the idea of becoming a book, but of spreading the Word. By the end of the 4th century A.D., with Christianity finally so potent a force that the Roman emperor had become a convert, a definitive Latin edition of the Bible was in order, and the books we recognize today were included, while

A point already made in our pages, and to be explored further in the pages that follow as well as right here: Jesus is shown to us as a Jesus we might know. He was, of course, born to a Semitic family, yet here He was rendered by Anthony van Dyck in the first half of the 17th century for a western audience that loved Him already, and would do so all the more upon seeing Him here with his mother, looking quite like the tow-headed European infant next door.

29

other letters, lectures and even gospels were disregarded. (The Book of Thomas, the most famous of the Gnostics and perhaps the first, was written in the 2nd century and so would have been purposely excluded.) This final group of books and the story it told became, for the burgeoning congregation that was and is Christianity, the authoritative version. The divinely inspired truth.

We note all of this now, rather than in our later chapter on the early years of Christianity, by way of indicating the basis for the story soon to unfold.

And now we backtrack to King Herod the Great, and the birth of Mary and Joseph's son.

SOLOMON AND HEROD LIVED AND RULED nearly a millennium apart, yet they seem connected—connected by the temple. Certainly much happened between Solomon's death in 930 B.C. and Herod's rise in the decades just before Christ's birth, but in biblical history they are events of secondary importance. With this crucial exception: A discord fomented by Solomon's often smart policies led to a split in the Israeli kingdom.

Jeroboam led the revolt against Solomon's

DENIS WAUGH (2)

Above: This is a grotto near Bethlehem. It was perhaps in a spot quite like this that Mary gave birth to her child after learning that there was no room at the inn. Here, she and Joseph hunkered down. Others took notice, according to the Gospels. At left is the Field of the Good Shepherd near Bethlehem. LIFE sent the photographer Denis Waugh to the Holy Land to depict for readers what these places might have looked like at the precise time of the Nativity. Bethlehem and Nazareth are much larger cities today, and yet there are precincts that hearken to antiquity.

successors and, when the kingdom was divided in two, he came to lead Israel, to the north. Solomon's son Rehoboam was put in charge of Judah, to the south. These two Hebrew states would wage war with each other and elsewhere, and were weakened by revolts and unrest for centuries. Egypt invaded, Assyria invaded, Babylonia, as previously noted, invaded (and destroyed Solomon's temple). And then, by the 1st century B.C., Rome came to rule all.

In 37 B.C., Rome installed Herod, who was only 36 years of age at the time but was soon to be known as Herod the Great. His kingdom included what had been Judaea, Idumea, Galilee and other contiguous lands.

He was ruthless, paranoid. He had, at one point, his wife and then his mother-in-law put to death; later, he had two of his sons killed. But he's remembered best for two other things. First, for rebuilding Jerusalem's temple on a fantastic scale. Herod's portico of the Second Temple extended some 800 feet. It had 162 Corinthian columns, stood as high as 100 feet, and had a staircase leading to walks, pools and gardens below.

And Herod is finally remembered best for his role in the Nativity narrative of Jesus Christ.

Soon enough, there would be a herald out there, in the land ruled by Herod and his sons. His name was John. Among his community of fellow Jews, prophecies were part of tradition, but there was no urgent time frame for their fulfillment. Now came

On this page and the following two, we see how artists adapt the story so that their audience might understand and be moved. This is a depiction of the Nativity by Pieter Brueghel the Younger, the Flemish painter of the late 16th and early 17th centuries. He realized that, to bring the Christmastime event home to his people, the village needed to be familiar, and the village needed snow.

On these pages, renderings of Mary and Jesus—all the same Mary, all the same Jesus. Above, left, a detail from an 18th- or 19th-century Ethiopian triptych entitled "Enthroned Virgin with Child and Angels." Right: "Virgin and Child," by an unknown Asian artist. Opposite: "Madonna on the Half-moon," an 1803 work from Mexico, created using feathers.

John, however: a phenomenon, who took his crusade to the wilderness. He dressed like, and proclaimed salvation for, the poor, shouting about the coming of their judge with a sense of imminency. He "preached, saying, There cometh one mightier than I after me, the latchet of whose shoes I am not worthy to stoop and unloose."

John's place of business was the Jordan River, to which he drew the masses for a ritual with which he would become exclusively associated: baptism, a cleansing by waters of all sin, a preparation for judgment. John said it was not enough to be descended from Abraham; salvation could only be gained by a conscious act of repentance and faith.

Christ would be baptized there by John: "Jesus, when he was baptized went up straightway out of the water . . . And lo a voice from heaven, saying, This is my beloved Son, in whom I am well pleased." But we will get to all that, after Jesus has arrived.

A JEWISH CARPENTER'S SON BORN TO HUMble circumstances, Jesus was descended from Abraham through the line of Isaac as it extended through David—so says the New Testament. As previously noted, the similarities between David and Jesus are pronounced: Both came from modest station, and both were of people who called Bethlehem, in the hills near Jerusalem, home. However, Joseph and Mary, Jesus's parents, had clearly moved away at some point, as Joseph's carpentry was in Nazareth. At that time, Nazareth was a modest, even overlooked village of roughly 200 families in central Galilee, clear across the Judaean wilderness from Jerusalem. Today, Nazareth is Israel's largest Arab city, with a bustling inner city; back then, it was the hinterlands.

In Nazareth, Mary received the Holy Ghost and became pregnant. Joseph, in a dream, was visited

by the angel of the Lord, who spoke to him of his wife's condition, saying, "And she shall bring forth a son, and thou shalt call his name Jesus: for he shall save his people from their sins . . . Then Joseph being raised from sleep did as the angel of the Lord had bidden him, and took unto him his wife."

Before Mary could give birth, the Roman ruler, Caesar Augustus, proclaimed that all people must register in the city of their origin (for what scholars now say was either a tax or a census). A simple tradesman like Joseph and his wife would never have dreamed of disobeying such an edict from on high, and so, despite Mary's state, they prepared to leave their home in Nazareth.

On Christmas, when much of the world celebrates the birth of Jesus, little thought is given to Joseph and Mary's arduous 100-mile journey from Nazareth to Bethlehem. The Gospels provide few details, but research by archaeologists and biblical scholars enables us to envision the route taken by the couple through the Holy Land. By the end of the first day of their odyssey, they would have passed the Sea of Galilee, which would be the

Opposite: The Roman client-king of Judaea, the madman Herod the Great, is seen in a 14th-century Byzantine mosaic giving the Magi their orders, which they will not obey once they have found Jesus. A quick note to forestall any future confusion: This Herod, who died in 4 B.C., which in fact might be the year of Christ's birth, is the one who figured in intrigues surrounding the Nativity. One of his sons, Herod Antipas, who would be tetrarch of Galilee after Herod the Great's death, was minimally involved in the events of Jesus's Passion. Below: The Magi followed a star, tradition holds, all the way to this shepherd's field outside Bethlehem, then found their way to Mary and the manger.

35

Nazareth, then and now. It was a village not well thought of by those who would write about Jesus. In John's Gospel, Nathaniel asks, "Can anything good come out of Nazareth?" even though he knows Jesus is said to have come from there. Perhaps, though, as mentioned in our text, Jesus was of the Nazarene sect, and not a native of the small and unimportant village? Regardless, the sticking points are that Joseph and Mary were "of" Nazareth; Jesus was eventually rejected by the locals (all four Gospels in the Bible and the famous apocryphal text the Gospel of Thomas include, vis-à-vis Nazareth, "a prophet is not without honor except in his own country"); and Jesus had to leave the rural backwater that was Nazareth in order to build his flock. Today, Nazareth is of course a site of religious pilgrimage, and despite being Israel's largest Arab city (far more than half its urban population of 64,600 is Arab), it has a distinct, if small, Christian populace. That is the Church of the Annunciation in the center of the photograph opposite, located, it is said, on the site where an angel told Mary she would bear the child Jesus. Apropos of nothing, Nazareth has been called the Silicon Valley of the Middle East for all the high-tech start-ups there.

setting for many dramatic chapters in their son's remarkable life. (Thirty years after His parents skirted the sea, Jesus would preach the Sermon on the Mount there.) On the fifth day of their journey, Mary and Joseph trekked westward through the Judaean Desert, a treacherous wilderness populated mostly by Bedouin shepherds. Its dangers included mountain lions, vipers, scorpions and marauding bandits. As the two approached Jerusalem, they likely confronted gruesome evidence of Roman tyranny—such as burned villages and toppled crosses that had been used to crucify rebellious Jews. For these pilgrims, however, the hardships of the road melted away the moment they entered the city. An ancient psalm well describes the spiritual elation that devout Jews like Joseph and Mary would have experienced when they first came to the summit of the Mount of Olives, and gazed upon this holy citadel: "Let my tongue cleave to the roof of my mouth; if I prefer not Jerusalem above my chief joy."

In the Field of the Good Shepherd, an angel of the Lord is believed to have announced Jesus's birth to the shepherds. It should be noted: Some

biblical scholars doubt that Jesus was born in Bethlehem at all, thinking Nazareth more likely for a Nazarean and noting that the sanctification of Bethlehem seems too convenient a way to fulfill a prophecy that the Messiah would come from Bethlehem. But the two Gospel writers who deal with the birth both say Bethlehem, and throughout the Christian world Bethlehem is viewed as the place where Jesus's life and saga began. The most famous and moving account, in Luke's Gospel, of course should be quoted here:

And there were in the same country shepherds abiding in the field, keeping watch over their flock by night.

And, lo, the angel of the Lord came upon them, and the glory of the Lord shone round about them: and they were sore afraid.

And the angel said unto them, Fear not: for, behold, I bring you good tidings of great joy, which shall be to all people.

For unto you is born this day in the city of David a Saviour, which is Christ the Lord.

Opposite: "Presentation in the Temple," by Rembrandt, in which Mary and Joseph have brought their newborn son to Jerusalem to have Him received by the Jewish clerics. Below: Quite near where the scene with Mary, Joseph and the Jewish priests might have been enacted are the temple ruins at Temple Mount, right beside the Al-Aqsa Mosque.

Unto You Is Born This Day

And this shall be a sign unto you; Ye shall find the babe wrapped in swaddling clothes, lying in a manger.

And suddenly there was with the angel a multitude of the heavenly host praising God, and saying,

Glory to God in the highest, and on earth peace, good will toward men.

The writers Luke and Matthew record events immediately following the Nativity as well. Luke says that some time after their boy's birth, Joseph and Mary returned to the temple in Jerusalem and, in accordance with tradition, sacrificed two more turtle doves to the Lord in thanks for their son. Then they struck out once more into the Judaean wilderness, toward home. The Gospel of Matthew has it quite otherwise, with Joseph being warned by God of Herod's wrath and fleeing with his family, at the Lord's instruction, into Egypt. "And was there until the death of Herod: that it might be fulfilled which was spoken of the Lord by the prophet, saying, Out of Egypt have I called my son." Again, some modern scholars see this extra excursion as being simply too neat a way to satisfy a prophecy, but the notion of the dastardly and violent Herod looming over Jesus's birth is certainly a dramatic one.

Other famous players in that particular drama were the Magi—the three wise men—who followed a star. These men of position had been sent by Herod to Bethlehem to investigate rumors about a strange and wondrous birth there. Find this infant king, said Herod, "and when ye have found him, bring me word again, that I may come and worship him also. When they had heard the king, they departed; and, lo, the star, which they saw in the east, went before them, till it came and stood over where the young child was." After their audience with Jesus and Mary, the three were warned by God in a dream that they should not report back to Herod, who certainly meant to have the child killed. And so "they departed into their own country another way."

And thus were Mary and Joseph left with their child—who was, for a time, safe.

MATT MOYER/CORBIS

Was there a flight to Egypt by Joseph, Mary and their young son? Did they then return to Nazareth across the Sinai Peninsula, seen here? The canonical Gospels are not in accord, but the essence of their shared story is consistent: Joseph and Mary's was a beleaguered family, and Jesus's would be a renegade life.

THE CHILD WAXED STRONG IN SPIRIT

At left is the 17th-century painting "Saint Joseph the Carpenter," by Georges de la Tour, a French artist known for his candlelit portraits. In this case, the warmth of father and son is enriched. That Joseph was a carpenter or a Nazarene at all is assumed but unproven, and whether Jesus ever apprenticed is speculative. Nevertheless, a church was built in Nazareth over the site of what was said to be Joseph's workshop.

T IS IMPORTANT TO HAVE AN understanding of Jesus's times. Such an understanding lends context, and helps us appreciate just how extraordinary was His success in influencing others, and in establishing Himself as one worth being remembered.

The bare-bones New Testament account sees Jesus as the earthly son of a carpenter, seemingly ready to follow in the family trade but then showing a precocity for philosophy and teaching, lecturing even His elders and senior clerics. If His message offended some, it was alluring to others. He was, in an era crowded with prophets, soothsayers, doomsayers and Zealots, especially charismatic. Jesus always stood out, was always apart from the pack.

For many religion scholars, the nutshell version is too simple and even, at times, misleading. Robert Eisenman is professor of Middle East Religions and Archaeology and Islamic Law and the director of the Institute for the Study of Judaeo-Christian Origins at California State University, Long Beach, and a visiting senior member of Linacre College at the University of Oxford—as well as a blogger on religion for The Huffington Post. He is the author of several books, including *The Dead Sea Scrolls and the First Christians.* He explained to LIFE why he felt the biblical presentation of Jesus doesn't go nearly far enough: "All the New Testament documents about Jesus, except Paul's letters, have been rewritten and overwritten. If you want the real picture of what happened in Palestine in the first century, the place to go is the Scrolls, which miraculously survived in those caves. The Scrolls offer an unadulterated picture of Palestine, and these texts don't accommodate anyone. You don't get those speeches of Jesus like in the Gospels, where he spouts 85, maybe 90 lines of Pauline-Christian doctrine.

"In Gospel scriptures, written by Greeks overseas, Jesus walks around the Galilean countryside like it's a peaceful town in Greece or Italy or Asia Minor. If you read the historian Josephus or the Dead Sea Scrolls, this is not the atmosphere of the time. The Scrolls depict a Palestine seething with political revolution, discontent, warfare, crucifixions. Jesus is always referred to as being from Nazareth in Galilee, but that is a reinterpretation [by the Gospel writers] based on geography. Actually, 'Nazarite' and 'Galilean' are words for members of a political messianic group. The Scrolls indicate that the kind of group He would have been born into was dedicated to God in a very extreme, purist manner, with a large set of puritan regulations: vegetarianism, never eating unclean foods, particular bathing practices. I place Jesus, if He existed, among these groups—probably the cult that included James, the Scrolls' chief character and a man often seen as Jesus's brother."

Whether or not Eisenman is right about who Jesus was (or might have been), his description of the Middle East at the time of Christ is helpful. That Jesus and His teachings were allowed to emerge from such a volatile social milieu—that they stuck—is remarkable. It speaks to the extraordinary nature of the man and His words. There were all of these false prophets, and then there was a man who would change the world.

Jesus's thinking was not unorthodox; it was radical. At a time when there was not only strong-arm rule by kings but also, in the streets, greed, violence and lawlessness, notions of pacifism and charity were alien. The idea of giving one's cloak to a needy stranger—a brother, Jesus suggested—did not have much currency in Palestine before He existed. Even religions that would reject Him as the Son of God, including Judaism and Islam, would later admire many of His sociological theories. These rules for living were and remain exquisite, and in fact, many of Allah's teachings as rendered by Muhammad some 600 years later are not unlike those of Jesus in their compassion, selflessness and social unorthodoxy.

HE ORDERING OF A FULL-BLOWN PHILOS-ophy and the proselytizing would come in time. First, there was the boyhood, of which we know something but not much. Perhaps even here, at an early age, ideas were being formed and examples shown.

Before he passed away in 2007, the Baptist minister Jerry Falwell shared with LIFE a vision of young Jesus—His life and times—that feels far different from Eisenman's, one that was based on

The Child Waxed Strong in Spirit

the New Testament outline and on personal faith: "Jesus grew up in Nazareth in the home of His mother, Mary, and Her husband, Joseph, who was not His father. Joseph was a carpenter. I believe that He, Jesus, learned the trade of carpentry like any other Jewish boy would have in such a home. I believe that He ran and played with His friends as a child. I believe He enjoyed good food and fun, and frolicking with His buddies and pals. The Gospels say He grew in stature and in wisdom—at age 12 He confounded the wise men in the temple. I believe He developed physically and mentally in the same way as any other child, and yet stood above any other child."

The episode in the temple, to which Falwell alluded, is one of the most charming in the Bible, which is a book that has many incidents of intrigue, drama, action, violence and inspiration, but not an abundance characterized by charm. Of the Gospel writers, Luke is regarded by many as the most poetic, and it is fitting that his is the account here. The boy Jesus, raised by Mary and Joseph in

Nazareth, "grew, and waxed strong in spirit, filled with wisdom: and the grace of God was upon him. Now his parents went to Jerusalem every year at the feast of the Passover. And when he was twelve years old, they went up to Jerusalem after the custom of the feast. And when they had fulfilled the days, as they returned, the child Jesus tarried behind in Jerusalem; and Joseph and his mother knew not of it. But they, supposing him to have been in the company, went a day's journey; and they sought him among their kinsfolk and acquaintance. And when they found him not, they turned back again to Jerusalem, seeking him." There they discovered the boy in the temple, listening and questioning the adults. When Mary asked her son how He could have disappeared and upset His parents so, Jesus answered cryptically: "wist ye not that I must be about my Father's business? And they understood not the saying which he spake unto them."

Such understanding, were it ever to come, would take time. But it could well have been that Joseph and Mary knew early on that they had a

Above, left: Jesus, the dutiful son, sews, as His mother looks on. At right: Inside the Basilica of the Annunciation. In Nazareth, Joseph and of course Jesus have been recognized, but Mary has been venerated elaborately. Pilgrims have, for centuries, made their way to Mary's Well, and still today the Orthodox Church of St. Gabriel at that site is a place of pilgrimage.

The Child Waxed Strong in Spirit

philosopher and a moralist on their hands. Some apocryphal writings, such as the Infancy Gospel of Thomas, depict an energetic adolescent Jesus doing miracles and playing tricks and even getting into mischief, but in the four Gospels of the Bible there is only this one account, in Luke, regarding Jesus's boyhood. The episode in the temple, for it to have been handed down, must have made an impression on someone. Perhaps on Mary? Did she tell this story often, to friends and family?

Yes, certainly, it could have been created by the writer or writers behind Luke. But even if so, they were ascribing the boy's actions to one who, by prior reputation, must have been special—precociously intelligent and persuasive.

In any event, Jesus was not about to stop thinking. Or talking. And—crucially—as He grew older and went about His business, His credibility did nothing but increase. Harvey Cox, one of the nation's preeminent theologians, who retired from teaching at the Harvard Divinity School in 2009, once expressed his thoughts on this to LIFE: "Gandhi said that what he found most attractive about Jesus was that He wasn't just someone who taught it, as many of the Asian sages did. He did it, He actually lived it. He loved His neighbors, His enemies. He stayed among the poor. He was an exemplar of His own teaching."

Seen here is the 1879 painting "The Twelve-Year-Old Jesus in the Temple," by Max Liebermann. At right is the Synagogue Church in Nazareth, built by Christian Crusaders. Tradition holds that the chapel exists above ground that was the location of a Roman-period synagogue where Jesus first learned, prayed and later preached.

HE CAME TO SAVE SINNERS

HE AMERICAN FOLKSINGER Woody Guthrie saw things in a linear fashion in his song "Jesus Christ":

When Jesus came to town
All the working folks around
Believed what He did say.
But the bankers and the preachers
They nailed Him on a cross
And they laid Jesus Christ in His grave.

Halle, Hallelujah!

In a discussion with LIFE, the noted Bible scholar John Dominic Crossan had a more complicated, but not dissimilar, assessment of Jesus's message and its ramifications: "If He was just talking about a nice idea, I don't think peasants would have been interested and I don't think the Romans would have been excited. I don't think He would have got Himself crucified. So I do presume that He both said and did something. He crossed over the line from talk to action. I think what He was doing was creating a movement of empowerment for the peasants, telling them that this is what you must do. You must take your lives back into your own hands. You must learn to heal one another.

"I think healing is crucial for me to understand why peasants are listening to Jesus. He demands that they share their food together, which might not seem much to us, but might seem much to an impoverished peasant who just lost his land. Jesus declares that that is what the Kingdom of God is like: Open healing and open eating together, an attempt to rebuild the peasant community from the grassroots upward. And the statement is that they are all empowered to do it.

"Jesus doesn't settle in one place and send messengers out to bring everyone back to Him. He sends people out to dress like Him and to act like Him, and to preach the Kingdom of God. He

RICHARD T. NOWITZ

For Jesus, all roads led to Jerusalem, in particular this one (opposite), which wound from the heights of the Mount of Olives down to the Kidron Valley and then up again to the temple (in the background is the Golden Gate on the east wall of the temple). Above: A man rides a donkey through the Old City, just as Jesus once did.

He Came to Save Sinners

doesn't have a monopoly on it. That is why I use the word 'empowerment' rather than 'domination.' I'm not even keen on the word 'disciples,' because in Greek it means a student of a teacher, and so the analogy is always master Jesus and his students. I would prefer to talk about Jesus's 'companions,' because that is what the message is, as I understand it. 'I do not have a monopoly on the Kingdom of God. Go and do likewise.'

"The people whom Jesus sends out are sent to heal and to teach just like Him.

"'Jesus the Sage' must come second. The healer has to come first, because if you're dealing with peasants you're dealing with the body. Peasants begin with their bodies. They want to know what the Kingdom of God does for my body. What does it do for bread and debt, to pick up on two things mentioned in the 'Our Father'? What does it do about daily bread, and what does it do about forgiveness of debts, which are the two ancient ghosts that haunt the peasant imagination?"

Certainly Jesus would find a welcoming audience among the very poor when He counseled them on how they might help themselves—and each other—in this hard life. Counseled them and then proceeded, as Gandhi rightly observed, to lead by example. "It's hard not to see the spiritual dimensions of what He said and did when you realize He was not trying to accumulate anything for Himself," Robert Funk, coauthor of *The Five Gospels: What Did Jesus Really Say?* and cofounder of the Jesus Seminar, a controversial think tank of scholars focused on the historicity of Jesus, told LIFE before his death in 2005. "He never saved up for a rainy day. He lived entirely out of God's providence, and said that others who wanted to be around Him should do the same."

But it wasn't all about better days on earth; it could not possibly have been. The message concerning God's providence had another crucial and thoroughly spiritual component, put succinctly by Jesus in Matthew's Gospel: "For what is a man profited, if he shall gain the whole world, and lose his own soul?"

WHERE WERE ALL OF THESE FINE WORDS and compelling thoughts, in whatever their original iterations and eloquence, sown? And who were these "companions" Professor Crossan speaks of? How did Jesus find them?

The biblical Gospels sketch a biographical narrative, but it must be pieced together.

As mentioned earlier, Luke and Matthew record the Nativity in their Gospels; Mark and John, by contrast, do not. They begin instead with John the Baptist, who himself was "not the Light" (the Gospel of John tells us) "but was sent to bear witness of the Light." John the Baptist was an itinerant preacher perhaps related to Jesus's family who

Above is a Piero della Francesca painting made circa 1450, "The Baptism of Christ." At right is the source of the Jordan River in Israel. It was in these waters that John baptized Jesus, the man who, John predicted, would fulfill the ancient prophecies that, many Jews hoped and believed, had been pointing to John.

may have been influenced by the ascetic Essene sect, which anticipated an imminent apocalypse and prepared for it by stressing baptism. John took pains to emphasize to his growing legion of followers that he was not the preordained Messiah, and that someone would follow him who was greater by far. He baptized Jesus in the River Jordan perhaps around A.D. 26 and was shortly thereafter arrested for his very public ministry and beheaded.

Jesus is, in the New Testament, the one foretold by John. After His baptism, He gained in spiritual power, which was fortuitous for He next was

tempted by the devil, who showed Him kingdoms to come. But Jesus resisted, and was now ready to start His own evangelical mission in Galilee.

He lectured in synagogues. According to Luke, Jesus's hometown congregants in Nazareth rejected Him, and He took His preaching to villages on the western shore of the Sea of Galilee. There He began building a team of disciples, starting with two pairs of brothers, all fishermen: Peter and Andrew, John and James ("I will make you fishers of men"). Jesus's flock was becoming well known in the region, and since there was some talk of His

Opposite is the altar in Cana's Church of the Miracle, which stands upon what is said to be the site of Jesus's first recounted miracle in the New Testament: turning water into wine. Above: A circa 1530 depiction of the miracle of the loaves and the fishes.

being the one presaged by John the Baptist, there
was a growing urgency for Him to prove himself—
not least to His lieutenants.

One day in Cana, a village north of Nazareth,
Jesus and His mother were attending a wedding.
When the wine ran out, Mary brought the news to
Jesus. Jesus ordered "six waterpots of stone" filled
with water. He promptly turned the liquid into
wine. In a later episode at Cana, Jesus heard about
a dying boy and healed him. He was proving His
divinity.

Despite the early rejection in Nazareth, He was
still working near home; His was yet a local movement. The Sea of Galilee, 16 miles east of Nazareth,
is not a sea at all but a 64-square-mile lake in a
depression of the Jordan River (in fact, at more than
600 feet below sea level, it is the lowest freshwa-
ter lake in the world). In Jesus's day it supported
vibrant cities—Capernaum and Bethsaida each
had more than 15,000 residents—as well as many
smaller fishing villages. This is the place where

ALBUM/ORONOZ/ART RESOURCE, NY

RICHARD T. NOWITZ

Jesus's mission was nurtured: Five of the eventual 12 of His disciples were from towns along the shore (and Mary Magdalene came from a Galilean village as well); the great majority of His recorded miracles were performed by, or on, the sea. As said, it was here that He turned water into wine. Here, He turned five loaves of bread and two fish into a meal for many. Here, He calmed the waters; He even walked upon them. He preached here often and effectively. He used a fishing net to show what judgment day would be like, when all humankind would be gathered up. Nearby, He delivered to the multitudes the Sermon on the Mount, an ethical

Left: Green valleys and rich, blue sky surround the sacred Church of the Beatitudes overlooking the Sea of Galilee. Rising above the valley is the historic Mount of the Beatitudes, where Christian tradition holds that Jesus delivered His monumental Sermon on the Mount (depicted above in a painting by the Spanish artist José Moreno Carbonero).

He Came to Save Sinners

lesson for the ages: "Blessed are the meek: for they shall inherit the earth . . . Blessed are the merciful: for they shall obtain mercy. Blessed are the pure in heart: for they shall see God. Blessed are the peacemakers: for they shall be called the children of God . . ."

Eventually, as Jesus gained more and more followers and notoriety, word spread beyond Galilee: that He had performed these miracles, fed a multitude with meager rations, healed the sick. In the New Testament, these stories are not presented for their supernatural effect but rather to forward a moral point or to instill faith. In their day, they certainly rallied Jesus's disciples, who started whispering, "He's the one." Such views, spread sotto voce, made life more dangerous for all concerned.

TODAY THE SMALL VILLAGE OF BETHANY, on the outskirts of Jerusalem, is known by the Arabic name el-Azariyeh, meaning "place of Lazarus." The town's Church of Lazarus is also named for Jesus's dear friend.

Jesus, His mission spreading and encroaching upon Jerusalem from Galilee, visited Lazarus and his sisters, Mary and Martha, several times at their house in Bethany; in fact, Bethany is sometimes referred to as Jesus's Judaean home. When, at one point, the sisters informed Jesus, "Lord, behold, he whom thou lovest is sick," Jesus quickly determined to go and help Lazarus. His disciples were concerned and warned against the trip, as Jesus's growing ministry had been making fresh enemies: "Master, the Jews of late sought to stone thee; and goest thou thither again?" Jesus insisted, "Our friend Lazarus sleepeth; but I go, that I may awake him out of sleep."

He did go, and He did raise the dead Lazarus and restore him to life. (He did, even if only metaphorically. John Dominic Crossan again: "I don't believe anyone has ever been brought out of the tomb who was dead. So the big question for me, when I read the Lazarus story, is—Why on earth are people telling this story? The only explanation that makes sense to me is that as far as these people were concerned, Jesus was bringing the dead back to life.") But Jesus, as the Gospels tell us, did not do Himself much good with this extraordinary act: "Then many of the Jews which came to Mary, and had seen the

Capernaum, called Kefar Nahum in Hebrew, was an ancient fishing village of 1,500 people located on the northwestern shore of the Sea of Galilee. It was the site of several of Jesus's miracles, and a church there is built on a spot where Saint Peter's house supposedly stood. The synagogue seen in this photograph was built in the 3rd century A.D., even as Christianity was on the rise in the Holy Land and in Rome.

The harsh terrain of Judaea, particularly between Jericho and Jerusalem, was the setting for climactic chapters in Jesus's mission. Outside Jericho, He healed one, perhaps two blind beggars and inspired a tax collector to repent his dishonest deeds. Between Jericho and Jerusalem, said Jesus, a good Samaritan came to the aid of a Jew who was stricken. Many in Jesus's Jewish audience would have hated Samaritans, but with Jesus, always, even in the face of hostility: compassion.

He Came to Save Sinners

things which Jesus did, believed on him. But some of them went their ways to the Pharisees, and told them what things Jesus had done . . . If we let him thus alone, all men will believe on him: and the Romans shall come and take away both our place and nation." Things were getting hot for Jesus, and they were getting hottest whenever He ventured near Jerusalem. Installed in that city by this time was the Roman governor Pontius Pilate. He was hearing the news, as were the Jewish prelates, and perhaps started to pay attention.

In John's Gospel, Jesus traveled to Jerusalem at least five different times during His career. Before the final journey, something extraordinary happened in the center of Galilee, on a mountain just outside the city of Capernaum. Jesus had drawn aside three of His disciples and asked them to accompany Him to a mountaintop (traditionally thought to be Mount Tabor). There, they prayed, and as they did so, Jesus was transformed—*transfigured* is the word the Bible uses to describe what occurred. He

Above: "The Resurrection of Lazarus," a 19th-century painting by Leon Bonnat. Right: Not far from Jerusalem, the Tomb of Lazarus, where Jesus raised His friend from the dead. The healing miracles were being recounted by His growing band of followers, and now this: Resurrection, life itself.

glowed, and then was visited by Moses and Elijah, who talked to Him. Then there came a cloud, and from the cloud a voice: "This is my beloved Son: hear Him."

And then it was over. The men descended, and Jesus asked His friends to keep what they had seen secret until the "Son of man" had risen from the dead.

What did the Transfiguration of Jesus mean? What does it mean today? Certainly it was yet another miracle that should have alleviated any lingering doubts about Jesus's divinity that Peter, James or John might have harbored. But in Luke's Gospel there is one thing more. Luke wrote that Moses and Elijah "spake of his decease which he should accomplish at Jerusalem." These words presage the Passion of Jesus that lay ahead in the not-distant future. They also clearly imply that this man was on a holy mission—an assignment—that would need to be *accomplished*. He came, or was sent, to save sinners.

Another of Jesus's most well-known miracles occurred outside Jericho, also not far from Jerusalem. En route to the Judaean capital as Passover was approaching—this time, to meet His ultimate fate—Jesus, traveling with His disciples, either paused on His way into the city to heal a blind man by the side of the road (according to the Gospel of Luke), healed the man upon exiting the city (says Mark) or healed not one but two blind beggars (according to Matthew). Only in Mark is the blind man given a name, Bartimæus. The differences are insignificant, as the moral of all three tellings is the same: Because a blind man believed in Jesus, because he considered Jesus divine, he was rewarded by the Son of God. As Jesus put it eloquently in Mark, "thy faith hath made thee whole." In that Gospel account Jesus finally told the man to "Go thy way," but, significantly, the man immediately fell in with Jesus's followers and proceeded with them on the Jerusalem road.

How large was Jesus's legion when it entered the great city in the week before the feast? That is unspecified, but clearly it was not just Jesus and the 12 disciples, and clearly this troop would have caused an immediate stir. In all of the Gospels, the action begins to speed up considerably at this point. The dramatic events of the Passion of Jesus Christ represent a crescendo like no other.

SCALA/ART RESOURCE, NY

Opposite: Mount Tabor in Israel's Jezreel Valley, 11 miles west of the Sea of Galilee. Christian tradition holds that it was here that Christ was transfigured before His astonished apostles. Above: "Transfiguration," by Mario Balassi (1604–1667).

AND ON THE THIRD DAY
HE ROSE AGAIN

SCALA/ART RESOURCE, NY

ANY WHO HEARD THAT JESUS was arriving rushed out to meet Him "and cried, Hosanna: Blessed is the King of Israel that cometh in the name of the Lord." Jesus, seeing the glorious city stretching out before Him, wept. This is the account of His arrival in Jerusalem, as told in the Gospel of John.

Mark, by contrast, is succinct in the extreme, and depicts difficulties arising immediately. "And they come to Jerusalem: and Jesus went into the temple, and began to cast out them that sold and bought in the temple, and overthrew the tables of the moneychangers, and the seats of them that sold doves; And would not suffer that any man should carry any vessel through the temple. And he taught, saying unto them, Is it not written, My house shall be called of all nations the house of prayer? but ye have made it a den of thieves. And the scribes and chief priests heard it, and sought how they might destroy him: for they feared him, because all the people was astonished at his doctrine."

So Jesus was, here in Mark, experiencing a far different emotion than in John: anger, on behalf of Himself, His flock, and the establisher of "My house," the temple in which the blasphemy had occurred—who of course could only be God the Father. Jesus was quickly confrontational in

At left: Pilgrims and other people approach Jerusalem's Old City at the Damascus Gate, in the present day. Above: A 6th-century manuscript illustration shows Jesus and His followers chasing their fate as they enter Jerusalem in the week before the feast.

BERNAT ARMANGUE/AP

Today, the view from the Franciscan chapel called Dominus Flevit includes the Dome of the Rock. It is said in Luke's Gospel that when Jesus walked toward the city at this spot on the Mount of Olives, He beheld the temple and wept for its beauty, and for the doom He foresaw for the temple, the city and the Jewish people. Dominus Flevit translates from the Latin as "the Lord wept," and the church is shaped like a teardrop. Opposite: *A* mikve, *a ritual bath, found near the Temple Mount and dating approximately from the Jesus period.*

Jerusalem, proactively setting in motion whatever climactic events were to follow; He was fairly lunging toward the fulfillment of many prophecies. He was courting His fate, and seeking His own Father.

Peter A. Bien, professor emeritus at Dartmouth College and translator of Nikos Kazantzakis's *Saint Francis* and *The Last Temptation of Christ*, said during an interview with LIFE, "Jesus, to succeed, had to choose martyrdom. He had been a failure in all sorts of human enterprises. One was to convert everybody to love, to turning the other cheek. He was an abysmal failure at that. He was also a failure in His more militant role—scourging the moneylenders, and so forth. He changed nothing. So, basically, the only power He had at the end was the power of abdication. It's very, very important that Jesus chooses to die. That He wants to die. He links with this universal process—pure spirit, God—rather than try to resist it or pretend it does not exist. By abdicating, He paradoxically achieves a most spectacular success of integration. By willing His own crucifixion, with Judas's help, He brings into the service of good the most horrendous of the devil's instruments, death itself. All who came after Him would see what had happened, and would know what the lesson is."

Jesus, intent upon the lesson, continued to preach in parables, defying His enemies to take Him. They didn't, at first. But Joseph Caiaphas, the High Priest in Jerusalem, had determined that Jesus must go, and was watching events proceed, looking for his moment. Caiaphas and his fellow priests decided not to make their move "on the feast day, lest there be an uproar of the people." Rather,

One of the world's most famous artworks is this 1498 mural by Leonardo da Vinci, "The Last Supper." It depicts the final meal that Jesus shared with His 12 apostles near the end of His troubled, triumphant week in the city. The Christian traditions involving the Eucharist, or Holy Communion, derive from this meal, during which Jesus urged His disciples "to love one another as I have loved you."

"the chief priests, and the scribes sought how they might take him by craft, and put him to death."

By craft.

And craft's name, as Bien has just mentioned, would be Judas.

IN JERUSALEM, JESUS GREW INCREASINGLY anxious, tormented; He prayed and contemplated what would come next. He then returned to His friends, telling them during a supper that there was a traitor in their midst. Each disciple asked, "Is it I?" When Judas asked, Jesus answered, "Thou hast said." Jesus told them at this last meal that His death was imminent, and then the men went out from the room to the Garden of Gethsemane, where Jesus engaged in solitary prayer.

This Last Supper requires consideration beyond how it forwards the plot. The manner in which it is presented in the Gospels is purposeful, and has been profoundly effective for two millennia in setting Christianity apart. Jesus was not only continuing with His campaign of provocation in Jerusalem, He was upping the ante considerably. He was doing so with the first communion, as recounted here in Matthew:

"Jesus took bread, and blessed it, and broke it and gave it to the disciples, and said, Take, eat; this is my body.

"And he took the cup, and gave thanks, and gave it to them saying: Drink ye all of it;

"For this is my blood of the new testament, which is shed for many for the remission of sins.

"But I say unto you, I will not drink henceforth of this fruit of the vine, until that day when I drink it new with you in my Father's kingdom."

The Dead Sea Scrolls scholar Robert Eisenman explained to LIFE the purposeful shock inherent in these words: "The scriptures have Jesus at the Last Supper saying, 'Drink this, it is my blood, this bread is my body.' The people in Palestine would have been horrified by such a thing. Even symbolically, it was forbidden to consume blood. These are the trappings of Greek Mystery Cult ideology, which was very helpful to Paul in his missionary activities in Asia Minor, Greece and ultimately Rome—where these kinds of mystery ceremonies were a familiar thing, which always involved some conquest over death, entering the tomb of the

Above: The early 16th-century painting "Jesus in the Garden of Gethsemane," by Vittore Carpaccio. As Jesus prays and frets, His disciples, who have been asked to keep watch, sleep. The garden is at the foot of the Mount of Olives, a mountain ridge east of the Old City seen at right in a picture made late in the 19th century that shows the setting in a relatively undeveloped state. In the canonical book Acts of the Apostles, *Jesus ascends to heaven from the Mount of Olives.*

savior figure, consuming his blood in some way.

"Many of the details in the Gospels we should recognize as legends, created without any historical information, that say what a great, precious person Jesus was."

That is Eisenman's counsel, but in fact what actually transpired during that meal is important to Christians on the level of, say, what really happened in Eden or with Moses and the burning bush. What happened is important, but so is what was meant. As Eisenman said, the Gospel writers—and Paul—were convinced that Jesus was a great, precious person. He represented, in fact, our connection to God and salvation. And therefore the stories that emerged from the Last Supper were true and factual, for here was the true and factual Son of God. If the play was unfolding according to tradition, Greek or Palestinian or otherwise, that was not only unsurprising, it was to be expected. Tradition and prophecy were the lingua franca of the writers and their readers, whosoever these readers might prove to be then and down through the centuries.

Jesus, in the Garden of Gethsemane and

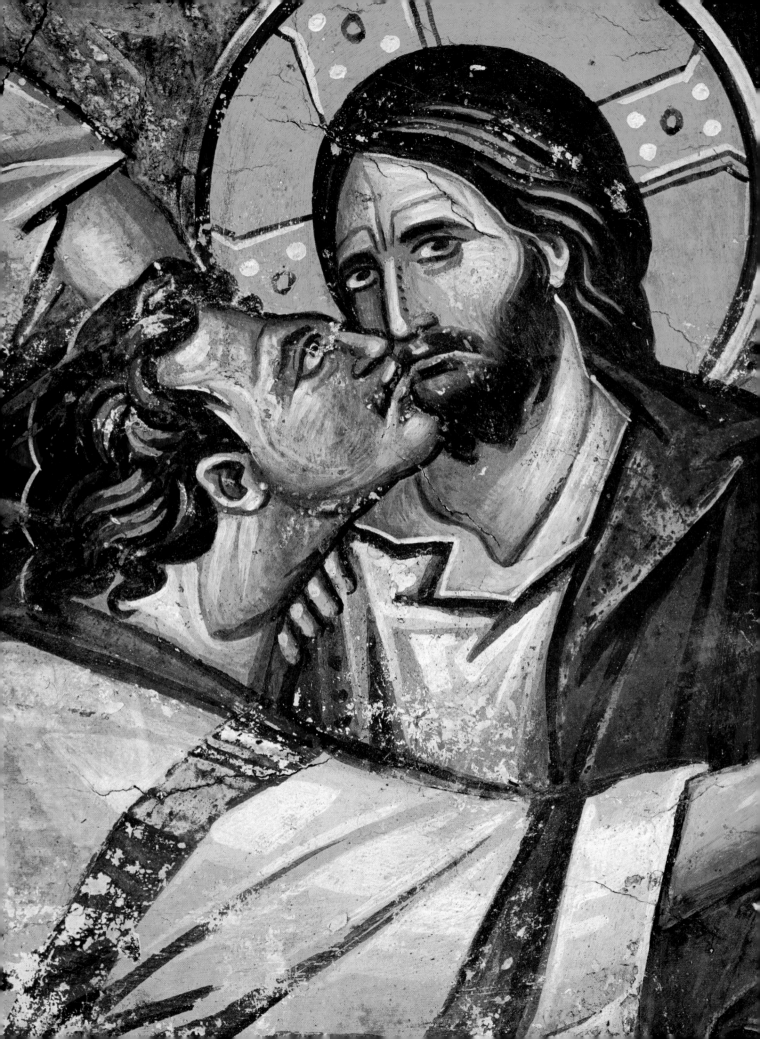

subsequently during His journey to death, experienced deep torment. In the garden, He wished to God that His fate could somehow be avoided, asking "that, if it were possible, the hour might pass from him. And he said, Abba, Father, all things are possible unto thee; take away this cup from me: nevertheless not what I will, but what thou wilt." The humanity (as opposed to the divinity) of Jesus is never more evident than in this meditation and then, shortly later, on the cross. Tyler Roberts, chair of the Department of Religious Studies at Grinnell College in Iowa and formerly of Harvard University, remembered to LIFE how these episodes impressed young people: "A lot of my students express questions about the troubled Jesus near the end of His life, when He felt He was being forsaken by God. To some this means He couldn't be the Son of God, because why would He, God, do that? For others, this was the most important thing in Jesus's life, because this showed the Son of God being most human. And the Son of God had to be human, because otherwise the message wouldn't make sense. It wouldn't mean anything for God to take human form unless God experienced this utter despair. Because that—the thing in the human condition that drove Him to this despair—is really what needs salvation."

Having finished His troubled discourse with God in the garden, Jesus woke His sleeping disciples: "Rise up, let us go; lo, He that betrayeth me is at hand. And immediately, while He yet spake, cometh Judas, one of the twelve, and with him a great multitude with swords and staves, from the chief priests and the scribes and the elders." Judas, working for Caiaphas, had arranged a signal with these guards—the one he would kiss was the one to be arrested—and immediately upon approaching Jesus, he betrayed Him.

S O NOW JESUS WAS IN CUSTODY. SUCH was the mysticism and attraction of His ministry—such was the potency—that He was treated with extreme care by the authorities. In Jerusalem, Pontius Pilatus (known in English-speaking realms as Pontius Pilate) was the fifth prefect of the Roman province of Judaea, serving in this era the Roman emperor Tiberius. Pilate would have liked to rid himself of the firebrand Jesus, and tried to move the case to the court

of another Tiberius employee, Herod Antipater, Herod the Great's son, known as Antipas, ruler of Pierea and Galilee—Jesus's territory. Antipas refused to involve himself in the issue, sending it back to Pilate.

Jesus was brought before Pilate, who asked, "Art thou the King of the Jews?"—a claim that would have been considered blasphemous. Jesus answered, "Thou sayest it. The chief priests accused him of many things: but he answered nothing. And Pilate asked him again, saying, Answerest

The dramatic events in the Garden of Gethsemane during Jesus's arrest are depicted here in frescoes showing Judas's betrayal, opposite, and, above, Peter cutting the ear of Malchus, servant of the Jewish High Priest Caiaphas. Jesus stays Peter's violence, heals the ear and is removed by His captors.

And on the Third Day He Rose Again

thou nothing? behold how many things they witness against thee. But Jesus yet answered nothing; so that Pilate marveled."

Pilate felt that the chief priests, whose authority was clearly being questioned by Jesus's very existence, had "delivered Him for envy." The governor of Judaea looked for a way out, and brought Jesus before the people of Jerusalem and asked if they wished for Him to be released. But the priests moved among the people, campaigning, and when Pilate asked, "What will ye then that I shall do unto him whom ye call the King of the Jews? And they cried out again, Crucify him." Pilate declared that he was washing his hands of the matter: that Jesus's fate and the responsibility for it lay with the mob and their priests.

Jesus was taken, tortured and forced to bear His own cross on the way to Golgotha in Jerusalem. Golgotha means "the place of a skull," and it has been speculated that its name referred either to Golgotha's being a skull-shaped hill, or perhaps to its use as a site of many executions. Three men were crucified that day: Jesus and, on either side, a thief. Jesus suffered grievously, at one point wailing, "My God, my God, why hast thou forsaken me?"

After the trials of Gethsemane, this is the second famous instance of Jesus's abject humanity—frailty?—that so intrigued Tyler Roberts's students, and that has been probed for 20 centuries by

Here are two wood tiles—"Christ Before Pilate," and "Pilate Washing His Hands"—from a series, **Episodes from Christ's Passion and Resurrection,** *done between 1308 and 1311 by Duccio di Buoninsegna. They are today part of the altarpiece in the Cathedral of Siena in Italy. The latter tile is a depiction of words from Matthew's Gospel: "When Pilate saw that he could prevail nothing, but that rather a tumult was made, he took water, and washed his hands before the multitude, saying, I am innocent of the blood of this just person: see ye to it." The source of Pilate's desire to avoid culpability in the death of Jesus has long been pondered by theologians. Did he fear God's retribution?*

And on the Third Day He Rose Again

theologians, historians, believers and nonbelievers. Speaking with LIFE several years ago, the late John Cardinal O'Connor of New York City summed up why, for the faithful of his flock, what happened on Golgotha was required to happen: "He's hanging there. People are spitting at Him, screaming, 'If you're the Son of God, prove it! Come down!' That's perfect common sense. But Catholics believe if He had come down from the cross He wouldn't have saved the world. This temptation to prove who He was: Of all His suffering, this was probably the worst."

In order to redeem humankind, He needed to suppress His divinity—at least while He finished the human part of His story.

ULTIMATELY, "JESUS CRIED WITH A LOUD voice, and gave up the ghost."

Today there is an ancient cave, cut from a rock in Jerusalem, that may have been the place where Jesus was laid to rest by His devotee Joseph of Arimathæa; as with many other biblical sites, we cannot know for sure that this is the right place, and indeed there are various candidate tombs in Jerusalem. But whether it was that cave or another matters little. What transpired at the tomb matters greatly.

The Stations of the Cross inside the Church of the Holy Sepulchre in Jerusalem, below, are glorious to behold, while the detail at right from Hans Memling's 1471 "Scenes from the Passion of Christ" is painful to see. For many centuries, the Holy Sepulchre basilica, also called by Eastern Christians the Church of the Resurrection, has been a place of pilgrimage in the Old City, as many believe it stands on the site where Jesus was crucified and was buried and then rose from the dead. Others hold that the Garden Tomb, which is elsewhere in Jerusalem and which we will see on the pages immediately following, is where Jesus was laid to rest.

And on the Third Day He Rose Again

DEAGOSTINI/GETTY

According to the Gospel of John, Mary Magdalene found the empty sepulchre. In Mark, which as we have mentioned is thought to be the first of the Gospels written, it was Magdalene, Mary (Jesus's mother) and Salome who found the stone rolled away. Then, continuing in Mark, it was to Magdalene that the resurrected Jesus first appeared.

She seems in these narratives altogether more strong and stalwart than the 11 remaining disciples (Judas having gone to die, perhaps by suicide, in grief). These male apostles didn't believe Magdalene when she told them Christ was risen. Women, including Magdalene and Mary, were also particularly noted by the Gospel writers for standing by Jesus during His ordeal on Golgotha. And, after all, it was one of Jesus's male followers who turned Him in for 30 pieces of silver, and it was the disciple Peter—hoping to save his own skin during the arrest of Jesus—who insisted that he knew Jesus not.

Whatever implications there might be about

the behavior of the loyal women as opposed to the men, the news they brought forth was astonishing: Jesus is resurrected. Jesus lives.

This has been imagined many times, and we will quote here, at our chapter's end, a wondrous passage from the essay collection *Miracles,* written by the Irish-born novelist (and convert) C.S. Lewis: "One has a picture of someone going right down and dredging the sea bottom. One has a picture of a strong man trying to lift a very big, complicated burden. He stoops down and gets himself right under it so that he himself disappears; and then he straightens his back and moves off with the whole thing swaying on his shoulders. Or else one has the picture of a diver, stripping off garment after garment, making himself naked, then flashing for a moment in the air, and then down through the green, and warm, and sunlit water into the pitch black, cold, freezing water, down into the mud and slime, then up again, his lungs almost bursting, back again to the green and warm and sunlit water, and then at last out into the sunshine, holding in his hand the dripping thing he went down to get. This thing is human nature, but, associated with it, all nature, the new universe."

The British artist Sir Edward Coley Burne-Jones began "The Morning of the Resurrection" in 1882 and completed it in 1886, at which point it was exhibited at London's Grosvenor Gallery accompanied by a quotation from John: "And when she had thus said, she turned herself back, and saw Jesus standing, and knew not that it was Jesus." The "she" is Mary Magdalene, who is visiting the empty tomb, and now sees the risen Christ, accompanied by two angels. The trio of female figures, earthly and ethereal, also brings to mind the women who stood by Jesus during His crucifixion, variously recorded in the Gospels and apocryphal writings, but often represented as Mary Magdalene; Mary, Jesus's mother; and Salome, sometimes identified as Mary's sister (and therefore Jesus's aunt) and in Roman Catholicism as Mary, mother of James, and therefore called Mary Salome—hence, "the Three Marys." The courage and loyalty of these women, especially in counterpoint to the behavior of some of Jesus's apostles during His crucial last hours, is striking.

Right: According to Luke, Jesus, on the day of His Resurrection, appeared to two of his disciples on the road to Emmaus, a town within 10 miles of Jerusalem. He spent time with them, and His second tour of earth in human form was underway. Even after most all of His apostles had been convinced of His Resurrection, Thomas doubted, and needed to be persuaded corporally; the moment was captured in a famous circa 1602 painting by Caravaggio, "The Incredulity of Saint Thomas" (opposite).

THE KINGDOM, THE POWER AND THE GLORY

HE RISE OF CHRIST'S CHURCH was begun with His returning from the dead, but while He had risen, He had not yet ascended, and so His Passion still had unfinished business—not least, convincing the doubting disciples of His continuing presence and influence in the earthly world. This was necessary because without their fervid belief in Him, there could be no evangelical movement. How could they spread the Word without faith in what had happened—and was, indeed, still happening?

According to Scripture, Jesus appeared to two disciples—one was Cleopas, the other perhaps was Luke—on the road to Emmaus on the very day of His Resurrection, having already been seen by Mary Magdalene. As they walked, Jesus lectured the men on how the recent events were in fulfillment of so much that had been predicted: "And beginning at Moses and all the prophets, he expounded unto them in all the Scriptures the things concerning himself." The men convinced Jesus to stay with them longer, and to break bread. Cleopas and Luke (if it was him) were overjoyed: "And they said to one another, Did not our heart burn within us, while he talked with us by the way, and while he opened to us the Scriptures? And they rose up the same hour, and returned to Jerusalem, and found the eleven gathered together, and them that were with them. Saying, The Lord is risen indeed."

These two who met Jesus in Emmaus can be considered, along with Magdalene, among the earliest Christian evangelists—those who would go forth, convincing at first the few and then the masses of the wisdom of Jesus Christ. The greatest, the most tireless, the smartest and by far the most effective of these would be Paul. He, with Peter, first grew the church. He was the one who led the spiritually hungry to Christ. And he—again, along with Peter—traveled the road to Rome.

N THE DAY OF HIS RESURRECTION, according to the Gospel of Luke, Jesus, having appeared first to Magdalene, then in Emmaus, then to Peter, addressed the congregation of 11 apostles in what is known today as "the upper room"—more formally Coenaculum or the Hall of the Last Supper, where Jesus's men gathered in private when in Jerusalem. As Jesus materialized there, the apostles were "terrified and affrighted," but Jesus "opened he their understanding." Then, in Luke, "he led them out as far as to Bethany, and he lifted up his hands, and blessed them. And it came to pass, while he blessed them, he was parted from them, and carried up into heaven."

In other Gospels, there are other appearances before the apostles. John records a visit with the 10 (Thomas was absent that evening), and then a second meeting in the same setting. In the interim, Thomas's brethren apostles had told him of Jesus's extraordinary visitation, "But he said unto them, Except I shall see in his hands the print of the nails, and put my finger into the print of the nails, and thrust my hand into his side, I will not believe. And after eight days again his disciples were within, and Thomas with them: then came Jesus, the doors being shut, and stood in the midst, and said, Peace be unto you. Then saith he to Thomas, Reach hither thy finger . . ." Doubting Thomas was thus convinced, and "Jesus saith unto him, Thomas, because thou hast seen me, thou hast believed: blessed are they that have not seen, and yet have believed."

The Gospel of John has a third appearance, when Jesus visited seven apostles by the shore of the Sea of Galilee, and a fourth was recorded by Matthew, who has Jesus materializing at an unspecified mountain in Galilee, instructing the apostles to go forth, "and teach all nations, baptizing them in the name of the Father, and of the Son, and of the Holy Ghost." At every turn, Jesus is actively promoting a dissemination of the Word.

What happened next was extraordinary—quite as extraordinary, if not as supernatural, as what had happened already. The acclaimed British writer Karen Armstrong, author of the seminal *A History of God,* among other books, and a former Roman Catholic nun, offered context during an interview with LIFE, even as she marveled: "To say that a man crucified in some corner of the Roman Empire was God was blasphemous in the Jewish world. Yet this unlikely idea, a complete nonstarter in religious terms, blossomed and became a great religion.

"Over the centuries, people have found God in Jesus in some way, so that there is a truth there. Religious people are pragmatic: They don't just believe things because they're told. If an idea doesn't yield some sense of life's ultimate meaning and value, they discard it. That's what we did when we decided we no longer wanted to be pagans. People found that the non-pagan way worked. I think people have found this with Jesus and Christianity."

Some sense of life's ultimate meaning and value: This is what Jesus's teachings represented for many as they were codified, edited and disseminated in the decades after His death and Resurrection. And Christianity, with the teachings at its core, would prove unstoppable.

This is a modern-day representation of what has been going on—first in secret, but for centuries in public—ever since John baptized Jesus and the Savior's flock began to grow: A Russian Orthodox priest performs baptisms in the Jordan River on the Jordan side of the Qasr al-Yahud Baptism Site where Orthodox Christians have come to celebrate the Epiphany on January 18, 2011. Qasr al-Yahud is believed to be the very place where Jesus Christ was baptized, and is a pilgrimage site on both the Jordan and West Bank (or Israeli) sides of the river.

The Kingdom, the Power and the Glory

SCALA/ART RESOURCE, NY

RICHARD T. NOWITZ

WHO TO CODIFY, EDIT AND DISSEMINATE, as well as parse and preach, these lessons? Would Jesus Christ's backers step up?

"The wondrous thing about Jesus is not that He was believed to possess such power that He attracted followers," Professor Shaye J.D. Cohen, a rabbi who has taught at Brown University and now Harvard, told LIFE. "The wondrous thing about it is that even after He was executed for being a troublemaker, His followers did not disappear. They did not just go away. Somehow, His death proved to be the catalyst for the emergence of something very new and very different, previously not seen in Judaism. It's impossible to find a similar group that grows up and endures so long after the death of its founding, inspirational figure. That's the wondrous thing: Not so much Jesus and His lifetime, as Jesus in His death."

Jesus's most effective proselytizer did not begin as any kind of follower, and the bare fact that the former Saul of Tarsus became an early Christian evangelist is nothing short of miraculous. Born into a strict Jewish family, Saul was a young Pharisee when he made his way to Jerusalem to study under a renowned rabbi. He was a strong student, and the fervency with which he pursued his Jewishness knew no bounds. This was in the early years after Jesus's death and, as His story attracted more and more attention, Saul became more fierce in his opposition. He would storm into private

Opposite: A Byzantine mosaic of Saint Paul's arrival at Neapolis, an ancient settlement on the Greek mainland founded by people from Thassos, an island off the Macedonian coast. Neapolis, which is where Paul landed in Europe for the very first time during his second missionary expedition, was also known as the Aegean seaport of Philippi, hence Paul's "Letters to the Philippians." Below: Much of his most famous work was done in Corinth, Greece, where he would have walked in the shadows of the Temple of Apollo (seen here), preaching a new and very different version of divinity.

In Cappadocia, Turkey, clandestine Christian churches arose among the rocks in the early centuries after Jesus's death. Monks and lay followers of Christ would gather here—and elsewhere throughout the Roman empire, where the free practice of religion was still forbidden—and hand down the teachings as they were being interpreted by evangelists such as Paul and the Gospel writers.

RICHARD T. NOWITZ

MENAHEM KAHANA/AFP/GETTY

houses to seize Jesus-followers and turn them over to jailers, "breathing out threatenings and slaughter against the disciples." The High Priest was impressed by Saul and gave him permission to go to Damascus and break up any Jesus cells there. Saul was a thug, and was sent out as a thug. But as Saul came near the city he was blinded by a light, and heard a pleading voice: "Saul, why persecutest thou me? . . . I am Jesus, whom thou persecutest . . . Arise, and go into the city, and it shall be told thee what thou must do." After three days of blindness, Saul was healed, baptized and enlisted in the cause of Christ. He slowly gained credibility with the disciples in Damascus and Jerusalem. Soon to be renamed (and become famous as) Paul, he embarked on his extraordinary mission.

The first of his three major tours took him to Antioch and Selucia, two cities on the Mediterranean island of Cyprus; and the second saw him visit, among other places, Athens. On to Corinth, another thriving port city in what is now southern Greece, where, in a temple that was already more than six centuries old, he enjoyed a success that had eluded him in Athens. He had made some few Athenian converts, to be sure, but had failed to found a church. In Corinth he convinced Jews and Gentiles alike of Jesus's greatness.

He began the habit, during his year and a half

Paul's letters to the Romans, Corinthians and Ephesians, among others, would change world history. Above are ruins on Curates Street, in Ephesus, Turkey, where the great evangelist once walked. Right: A nun enters Mary's House chapel in Selçuk, a mile northeast of Ephesus. In recent years, Pope Benedict XVI has celebrated Mass there, something of a bold (some said, provocative) gesture in a principally Muslim culture where Benedict's earlier comments on Islam had been criticized.

in Corinth, of promoting His mission elsewhere even as he evangelized on the ground: He wrote two letters to the Thessalonians, these being the New Testament's first Epistles of Paul. The letters were paternal, learned and theological. They were inspirational sermons, designed to keep the recently persuaded on track. Later, in his first of two letters back to the Corinthians, he wrote some of his most famous—and moving—passages: "For as the body is one, and hath many members, and all the members of that one body being many, are one body: so also is Christ. For by one Spirit are we all baptized into one body, whether we be Jews or Gentiles, whether we be bond or free; and have been all made to drink into one Spirit. For the body is not one member, but many . . . God hath tempered the body together, having given more abundant honour to that part which lacked: That there should be no schism in the body; but that the members should have the same care one for another. And whether one member suffer, all the members suffer with it; or one member be

honoured, all the members rejoice with it." Paul's ministry grew strong in Corinth, and then it was on to Ephesus.

"Paul is the real founder of Christianity as we know it," the late Robert Funk, cofounder of the controversial conclave of scholars called the Jesus Seminar, told LIFE. "Paul did not know Jesus. Apparently he had no use for information from Jesus, although he refers to His teachings a few times in his letters. He may actually have been in competition with the evangelists who produced the narrative Gospels. We don't know. We know Paul was in competition with the leaders of the Jerusalem church, founded by James, the brother of Jesus. We learn that from Paul's letters, among other sources."

Paul would, of course, win that contest.

THE SITE OF ANCIENT EPHESUS AND THE adjacent town of Selçuk, 30 miles south of what is now the Turkish city of Izmir, are rife with ruins from various periods, piled up on one another. There are remnant constructs implying the grandiose—the remains of the Temple of Artemis, built in the 7th century B.C. and counted among the seven wonders of the ancient world; a 6th-century basilica built by the Emperor Justinian—and then there is a modest stone building known as the House of Virgin Mary. It is said that Jesus's mother spent her senior years in Ephesus. Paul visited Ephesus twice, stopping briefly near the end of his second missionary journey, then spending more than two years here during his third and final mission. What happened this latter time says a lot about Ephesus and about the success Paul was having. The old town was still invested in the fertility goddess Artemis when Paul first visited, and local craftsmen saw their brisk trade in replicas and souvenirs for pilgrims threatened by Christianity's rise. They denounced Paul and staged an anti-Christian riot. Paul moved on from Ephesus dejected. But when he returned, he was welcomed, heralded. Times and attitudes had—very quickly—changed, no small thanks to Paul himself and his message.

During Paul's second visit to Corinth (part of his third missionary journey), he wrote to the Romans, saying he hoped to see them, adding at one point, "Bless them which persecute you: bless,

Left: Saint Peter. Right: The cave of Pan near one of the sources of the Jordan River in the vicinity of Mount Hermon in what was the ancient Roman city of Caesarea Philippi. Perhaps around A.D. 29, Jesus and his followers visited this area, as Mark told it: "Now Jesus and his disciples went out to the town of Caesarea Philippi; and on the road he asked his disciples, saying to them, 'Who do men say that I am?'" And Simon Peter confessed Jesus to be the "Son of the living God," whereupon, by tradition, Jesus "handed the keys" to Peter—designating him as "this rock" upon which Christianity would be built.

and curse not." He would soon be heeding his own admonition. From Corinth he went to Philippi, Assos, Miletus, Patera, back across the sea and eventually, against the advice of associates, once again to Jerusalem: "I am ready not to be bound only but also to die at Jerusalem for the name of the Lord Jesus." He nearly did die, at the hands of a mob, and was taken into custody. Paul claimed that as a Roman citizen he should be allowed to stand trial in Rome. The governor replied: "Hast thou appealed to Caesar? unto Caesar shalt thou go." Paul was transported in a ship that tried to hug the shore, but was blown out into the Mediterranean by a storm that lasted 14 days. The vessel wrecked off Malta, and the men spent three months on the island before being picked up.

Thus did Paul reach Rome, where he continued to assert the divinity of Jesus Christ. Accounts of his death vary—there's nothing in the Bible—but Christian tradition holds that he was beheaded, perhaps during the Emperor Nero's persecution of A.D. 64.

Meantime: Whither Peter? During His life on earth, Jesus had singled out His disciple Simon Peter for a very special role in the establishment of His church. He said Peter would be "this rock" upon which any future institution would be built, adding: "And I will give unto thee the keys of the kingdom of heaven: and whatsoever thou shalt bind on earth shall be bound in heaven; and whatsoever thou shalt loose on earth shall be loosed in heaven."

What Jesus did not presage was that the church would be built in Rome—in the very place where the emperor's awesome earthly empire was then headquartered.

Although, as with the case of Paul, there are no biblical accounts of Peter's fate in that city, early Christian evidence maintains that he did go to Rome, after a career as a leading Jesus disciple in the Holy Land. In that earlier role, he was influential in siding with Paul's opinion that Gentiles, too, should be recruited—not just Judaean Jews. He wanted an inclusive church, one that might grow large.

Certainly he would not see his dream realized. He, too, might have been martyred during Nero's persecution; according to an ancient tradition,

Peter was crucified on an inverted cross. Further tradition holds that his burial site is directly under St. Peter's Basilica in Vatican City.

It's notable that Rome was sending a message to Christians with the deaths of Peter and Paul, and to Jews with the sack, in A.D. 70, of the Second Temple in Jerusalem, within just a few years' time. Surely the proactive empire felt it had won the day. But faith is, by its nature, resilient. And the attractiveness of the lessons in scripture—in the Hebrew Tanakh and the Christian Bible—would prove durable. Rome could kill a man and even, for a time, a movement. It could overrun a state, as it did Judaea.

Peter, charged by Christ to forward His mission and church, took his cause to Jerusalem and eventually to Rome. There, according to Christian traditions, Peter was crucified by the empire (below), and his remains today are in a tomb beneath the Vatican (opposite). He is regarded by the Roman Catholic Church as first in a line of—so far—266 popes, having led the flock from the time of Christ's death for perhaps as many as 35 years.

But it could not erase the truth in the hearts and minds of those who believed.

In short: The emperor may have killed these first two Christian messengers, but he could not kill their message, and Peter and Paul can truly be looked upon as the founders of Christ's church. Clandestine congregations throughout the Holy Land, Turkey and on toward Rome became better organized and—slowly—more aboveground. Within only decades, Christianity had taken root, spread to Spain and elsewhere in Europe. Within

Opposite: Roman emperor Constantine the Great and his mother, Helena, are both regarded today as saints by many Christian faiths. The empress Helena was said to have worked among the poor and released many prisoners, perhaps setting an example for her son in what would come to be known in later ages as "Christian charity." Constantine, of course, allowed for religious tolerance throughout the Roman Empire and, before converting on his deathbed, moved his headquarters to a city in today's Turkey that would be named after him: Constantinople. There, in the city now called Istanbul, the splendiferous Hagia Sophia (below)—which was consecrated as a Christian basilica in the 4th century, later became a mosque and is today a museum—shows signs of its former lives in Christian iconography and Islamic calligraphy.

three centuries, after hundreds had been martyred and thousands had taken to praying daily on their knees to Jesus, it had grown strong, and now was to become mighty. The Roman emperor Constantine I—Constantine the Great—with his finger to the wind, signed the Edict of Milan in 313, ordering tolerance of all religions throughout the empire. He himself converted to Christianity on his deathbed, and thus sent his empire on its way to conversion, too. Constantinople became the headquarters of the Eastern Empire and of Orthodox Christianity, while Rome is where the Vatican rose.

There would, down the ages, be schisms and offshoots—the Lutheran fissure in Germany leading to the rise of Protestantism; various orthodoxies arguing with each other and with Catholicism; movements from the Jehovah's Witnesses to the Latter-day Saints. There would be travesties in Jesus's name, with the anti-Muslim Holy Land Crusades of the 11th through 13th centuries being an egregious example. There would be so much that never could have been foreseen.

All of it started with a man, then His dedicated followers . . .

And, always, with the Word.

*We talked in the caption on the previous page of the term **Christian charity**. There have also been, through the centuries, Christian atrocities—some of them done in the name of Christ and others in abuse of His teachings. On these two pages, we consider the Crusades, a series of brutal holy wars waged by the Catholic church against Islam. Below is a 15th-century depiction of a battle during the First Crusade, which rampaged through the Holy Land from 1096 to 1099 after being launched by Pope Urban II. The Crusader castle of Krak Des Chevaliers (right) is in Syria. It was a base of operations for the Knights Hospitaller in the 12th and 13th centuries, with a garrison of 2,000 at its peak.*

In our present day, Jesus lives here. Which of Michelangelo's masterworks in the Vatican is most awe-inspiring: Saint Peter's Basilica itself, his "Pietà" sculpture or, here, his ceiling of the Sistine Chapel? Perhaps in no other place in the world does the spirit sound so ringingly as at this altar. Jesus lives here . . .

HE IS ALL THINGS TO ALL MEN

IT WOULD BE AN ABSURD EFFORT to address, historically, the two millennia march of Christianity in a single chapter. Many libraries of books have been written on the subject. Individual volumes address this incident or that individual, this holy war or that one, this heroism in the name of Christ and that heresy, this pope and that anti-pope, this schism and that rapprochement, this interpretation and that reinterpretation and then the rebuttal and then the counter argument to the rebuttal. If one aspect of the story of Jesus is irrefutable, it might be this: He mattered greatly to His flock nearly two thousand years ago, and He matters greatly to many, many more—people sitting on both sides of the aisle—today. The 18th-century Scottish poet Michael Bruce put it quite beautifully in one of his Gospel Sonnets when commenting upon Jesus's constant connection with humanity in the years since His death:

> "In every pang that rends the heart
> The Man of Sorrows had a part."

Indeed. World history offers no other figure as affecting and, it can be argued, omnipresent as Jesus. His cause has had a billion and more adherents down the centuries, and many and virulent enemies. It has weathered tempests almost incomprehensible in their ferocity. We have already mentioned the Crusades, but realize: Jesus has been invoked, one way or another, in thousands of battles since, and what He might think of such cataclysms as the devastating world wars of the 20th century or the tragedy of September 11, 2001, is always a question. Famine in Africa, drought in the American Dust Bowl, tsunamis in Indonesia or Japan: What would Jesus do? How could prelates dedicated to Him have allowed—or perpetrated—rampant abuse of the most innocent, our children? Then too, didn't the Catholic charities rush to New Orleans in large numbers after Hurricane Katrina?

Adolf Hitler was raised a Christian.

Christianity gave us Mother Teresa and Billy Graham.

"Christianity," wrote Tolstoy, "with its doctrine of humility, of forgiveness, of love, is incompatible with the state, with its haughtiness, its violence,

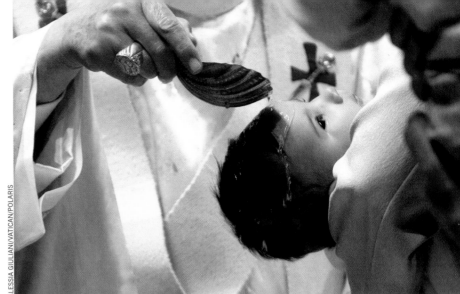

ALESSIA GIULIANI/VATICAN/POLARIS

CHRIS CURRY/JOURNAL STAR/ZUMA

JIM LO SCALZO/EPA/CORBIS

...And Jesus lives here. Left: In the James River in Henrico, Virginia, not far from where early settlers brought Christianity across the Atlantic and where, later, the North fought the South during the Civil War, the First Baptist Church of Richmond, Virginia, holds its annual River Baptism. Top: A baby is baptized in Rome by Pope Benedict XVI. Above: In Arthur, Illinois, two Amish girls hug following a baptism. Jesus lives here...

its punishment, its war." Perhaps surprisingly, Napoleon would not have argued. "Alexander, Caesar, Charlemagne and I myself," he said, "have founded empires; but upon what do these creations of our genius depend? Upon force. Jesus alone founded His empire upon love; and to this very day millions would die for Him." Bonaparte's 19th-century countryman, the poet and dramatist Alfred de Musset, went further: "Christianity ruined empires, but saved peoples."

We care in our country about our nation's thoughts and attitudes, and we always care to know, about almost anything, what the Founding Fathers felt. Listen, then, at a little length, to Thomas Jefferson, who considered Jesus deeply and often, and who took scissors to his personal copy of the New Testament, cutting out the miracles

He Is All Things to All Men

... *And Jesus lives here. Below: Despite threats of violence from nationalist groups, Orthodox worshipers attend the Virgin Mary service, celebrating her Assumption, led by Ecumenical Greek Orthodox Patriarch Bartholomew I at the ancient Sumela Monastery perched on the side of a cliff in northeastern Turkey. Right: An Easter prayer service at the Church of the Holy Sepulchre in Jerusalem's Old City is attended by pilgrims on the eve of Orthodox Easter. Far right: Early morning worshippers gather around Bet Giyorgis, the last of Ethiopia's stone churches to be built, carved out of the earth in a cruciform shape. Jesus lives here ...*

and pasting together the teachings for his daily edification: "To the corruptions of Christianity I am indeed opposed; but not to the genuine precepts of Jesus Himself. I am a Christian, but I am a Christian in the only sense in which I believe Jesus wished anyone to be, sincerely attached to His doctrine in preference to all others; ascribing to Him all human excellence, and believing that He never claimed any other . . . [Through Jesus] a system of morals is presented to us, which, if filled up in the true style and spirit of the rich fragments He left us, would be the most perfect and sublime that has ever been taught by man . . .

"The morality of Tacitus is the morality of patriotism . . . The universe was made for me, says man. Jesus despised and condemned such patriotism; but what nation, or what Christian, has adopted His system? . . .

"It is not to be understood that I am with Him in all His doctrines. I am a Materialist; He takes the side of spiritualism. He preaches the efficacy of repentance towards forgiveness of sin; I require a counterpoise of good works to redeem it, etc., etc. It is the innocence of His character, the purity and sublimity of His moral precepts, the eloquence of His inculcations, the beauty of the apologues in which He conveys them, that I so admire . . .

"The [United States'] bill for establishing religious freedom, the principles of which had, to a certain degree, been enacted before, I had drawn in all the latitude of reason and right. It still met with opposition; but, with some mutilations in the preamble, it was finally passed; and a singular

proposition proved that its protection of opinion was meant to be universal. Where the preamble declares, that coercion is a departure from the plan of the holy author of our religion, an amendment was proposed, but inserting the word 'Jesus Christ' so that it should read, 'a departure from the plan of Jesus Christ, the holy author of our religion'; the inserting was rejected by a great majority, in proof that they meant to comprehend, within the mantle of its protection, the Jew and the Gentile, the Christian and the Mohometa, the Hindoo, and Infidel of every denomination."

Even then, there was discussion and debate not unlike what we experience today about such measures. Jesus lost that argument, but most of Jefferson's fellow Founding Fathers, several of whom were Unitarians and shared his admiration of the philosophical Jesus rather than the miraculous Jesus, were uniform in their praise:

"It is impossible to reason without arriving at a Supreme Being," said George Washington. "Religion is as necessary to reason, as reason is to religion."

"Jesus is benevolence personified," said John Adams, "an example for all men."

"As to Jesus of Nazareth, my opinion of whom you particularly desire, I think His system of morals and His religion, as He left them to us, is the best the world ever saw, or is likely to see," said Benjamin Franklin, "but I apprehend it has received various corrupt changes, and I have, with most of the present dissenters in England, some doubts as to His divinity."

EVER THUS: THE ADMIRATION AND ARGU-
ing and the devotion and the questioning
and, for some, the qualms.

Much more recently than the late
18th century, LIFE went out again into America
to see where Jesus stood in the modern day. He of
course still held a place of primacy in many hearts
and minds. Even people who, having examined
matters while operating in the properly skeptical
world of scholarship, found themselves moved by
the man. At Dartmouth, our Kazantzakis scholar
Peter Bien, who was quoted earlier in these pages,
said eloquently, "The Gospel writers were creating
a moral tale around a real man—they had their
reasons. I realize much of what they wrote wasn't
literal history. I realize much of what we know
about Jesus is novelistic. But I act as if it isn't."

More observations worth considering:

"He was either who He said He was and that
He came to do what He said He came to do, or

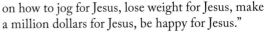

He was a liar and a deceiver," said Dr. C. Everett Koop, the former Surgeon General of the United States and a physician who believes that a patient's faith can help him or her keep a positive outlook and even abet the healing process. "Jesus's claims were blasphemy to the Pharisees, but became the foundation of a religion established by His followers, which has flourished for two thousand years. Millions of people today—by faith alone—accept the claims and promises of Jesus. Could such a continuing adherence to belief in these claims and promises be rooted in anything less than truth and integrity?"

"I don't see how, without the gift of faith, you would believe He was the Son of God," said the late John Cardinal O'Connor of New York City. "Faith makes the difference. You can study the Scriptures till your eyes fall out, and without the gift of faith you're not going to believe Christ was the Son of God. The miracle is faith itself."

"What most fascinates me is how Jesus is *used* by contemporary Americans," said Robert C. Fuller, author of *Spiritual But Not Religious: Understanding Unchurched America,* among other works. "Note, for example, the countless books in the born-again market written by beauty-contest winners, athletes, soap-opera stars, et cetera—who all claim Jesus helped them become celebrities. There are books

. . . And Jesus lives here. The world's meekest and mightiest answer His call, and on these pages are people we know. Opposite, top: Mother Teresa, the late Roman Catholic nun, ministers at her Missionaries of Charity in Calcutta, India, in the 1970s. Bottom: American Protestant evangelist Billy Graham preaches at Madison Square Garden in New York City in 1957. Below: Former U.S. President Jimmy Carter and his wife, Rosalynn, work on a house being built by the Habitat for Humanity organization in Washington, D.C., in 1992. Jesus lives here . . .

on how to jog for Jesus, lose weight for Jesus, make a million dollars for Jesus, be happy for Jesus."

"In a way, many of these athletes probably even identify with Jesus, for He was special and could astound onlookers with the stuff He did, too," said Frank Deford, the sportswriter and NPR commentator. "In sports, Jesus often seems to be more of a buddy than a savior. He's a good guy to have on the bench. The problem, of course, is that if you get too friendly with Jesus, then it's logical to expect Him to root for you and your team. Intellectually, sure, athletes know that Jesus doesn't give a hoot about any stupid game, but since they get so used to sycophants fawning all over them, it becomes easy for them to believe that, yes, deep down in His heart, Jesus is really cheering for their team."

"I know that some people don't think so, but I think Jesus was a feminist," said Susan Haskins, author of *Mary Magdalen: Myth and Metaphor.* "Early Christianity is a very different thing from the Christianity that we know of. Jesus cured ill women. He allowed them to become people who related His truths, like Martha of Bethany, and He forgave a repentant prostitute and told her to go away and sin no more, whereas the Pharisees were very negative about the prostitute, and rejected her, and implied that Jesus should not know her, that He should not allow her to touch Him because she was polluted. Yet He allowed her to touch Him. He forgave her."

"I find Jesus through prayer," said the techno recording artist Moby. "I try to read the Bible every day. I read the whole thing. I go through it page by page. The notion of Christ as my savior is not something I focus on. I would say that He is. Who knows what happens when we die? I have no idea. Christ says we become like angels, there are references, but I tend not to worry about it too much. I almost wish that life eternal wasn't part of the issue, because I sometimes feel that it's like dealing with an adolescent—I'll let you borrow the car if you clean the garage. I'd rather just clean the garage and not get into this system of doing things for rewards. I have an understanding of the universe as an unknowable but fascinating and wonderful place. I see human beings as part of that universe."

"I've been to Jerusalem three times," said the singer Aaron Neville. "I've made the pilgrimage.

It was a good feeling. I felt sorrow for Jesus, for what He had to go through. But I felt joy for Him having been born, and that He cared for me. I read a poem a long time ago, when times were hard for me, called 'Footsteps in the Sand.' This man was talking over his life with Jesus, who had promised that He would never leave him. Looking at his walk on life's beach, the man says, 'I see two sets of footprints in the sand for most of the time, when things are all right. But in my hardest times, when things were really dark and dreary, I see only one set of footprints. You promised you would never leave me.' And Jesus says, 'My son, I never did leave you. The times you see one set of footprints were the times when I carried you.' I carry that poem with me in my wallet."

"Matthew 5:48 says: 'Be ye perfect, even as your Father which is in Heaven is perfect,'" quoted the country singer Willie Nelson. "The purpose of life is to reach perfection. The rose starts as a seed or cutting, then grows and prospers with the sunshine and the rain. After a period of time, the perfect rose blossoms. The human experience is much the same, except the time span is much greater because man, before he can reach this state of perfection, must return again and again through many incarnations in order to conquer all disease, greed, jealousy, anger, hatred and guilt. In order to achieve perfection man must use his imagination to create an image of himself in his mind as a happy, healthy person, perfect in every way. He must pattern himself after the masters of perfection, such as the great master Jesus."

IN SUCH A MEAGER SAMPLING—A ROUND of phone calls, a few sit-downs—such a wide range of opinion on, and use of, Jesus.

One fact is overarching: Jesus today is not only present, He is potent.

It was in a quotation from the Gospel of Mark that a question was posed many pages ago in our book: Who do you say that I am? Many among us attempt an answer on a daily basis, wondering about Jesus, and ourselves in His image. Many others among us take solace in Jesus's promise as voiced in Matthew, which remains as yet irrefutable after two thousand years' time:

"And, lo, I am with you always, even unto the end of the world. Amen."

. . .And Jesus lives here, nearly half a world away from Jerusalem and the Holy Land and the grandeur of Rome's Sistine Chapel, a continent away from Virginia's James River baptisms, a far remove from the pain of Calcutta or the shouted amens of Madison Square Garden . . . Jesus lives here, in Ritzville, Washington, where a mother and daughter make their way to church. Jesus lives here.

Pietà

We opened our book with a detail of Jesus's face from Michelangelo's famous sculpture, which is housed at the Vatican. We return now to the entirety of the madonna-and-child masterwork. It reminds us that His was a human story—that was the point. In the astonishing beauty and power of Michelangelo's "Pietà," it hearkens to the spiritual as well.

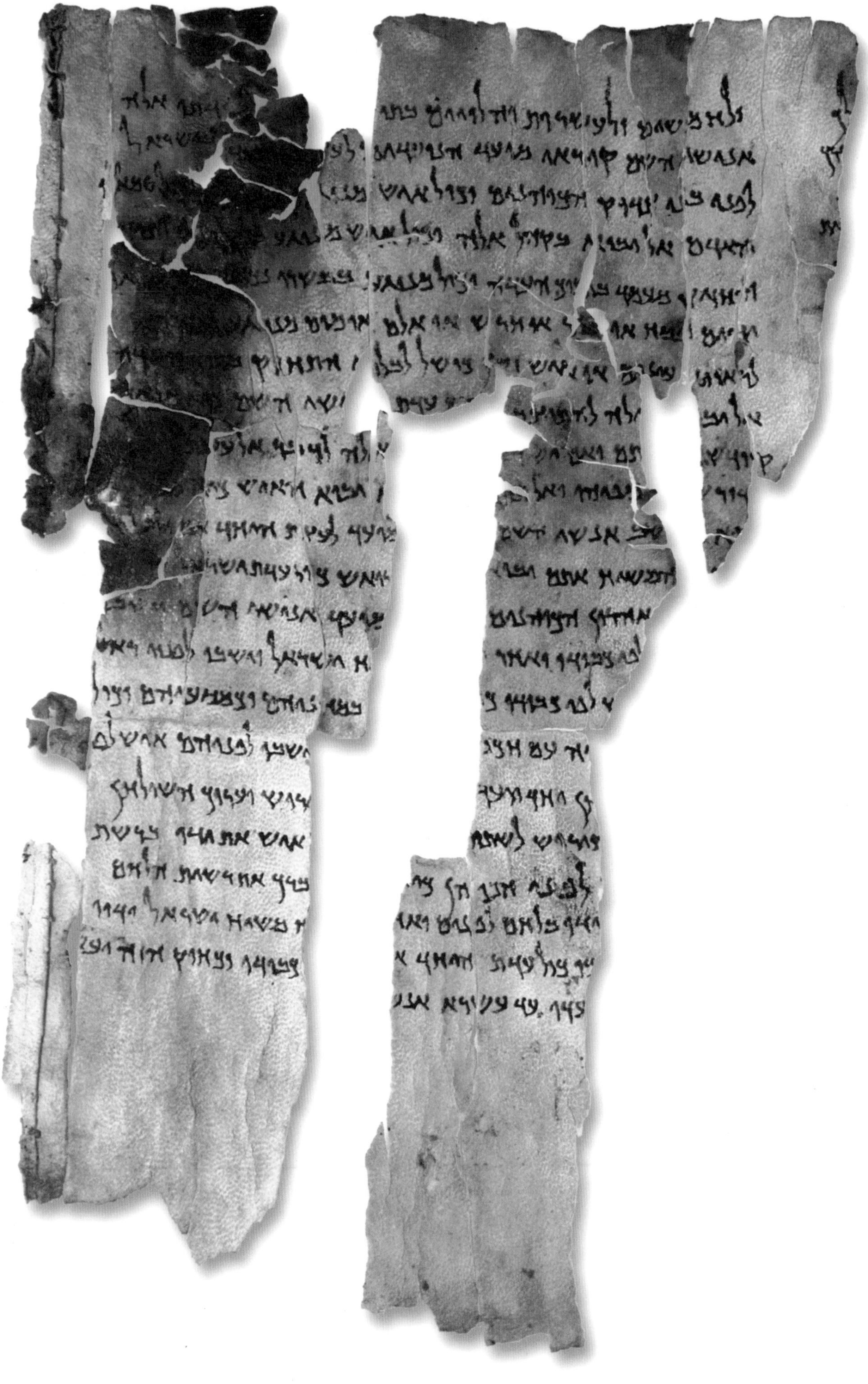